Principles
of Revival

Principles of Revival

Compiled & Edited by Louis Gifford Parkhurst, Jr.

Charles G. Finney

BETHANY HOUSE PUBLISHERS
MINNEAPOLIS, MINNESOTA 55438
A Division of Bethany Fellowship, Inc.

Published by Bethany House Publishers
A Division of Bethany Fellowship, Inc.
6820 Auto Club Road, Minneapolis, Minnesota 55438

Printed in the United States of America

Library of Congress Cataloging-in-Publication Data

Finney, Charles Grandison, 1792–1875.
   [Sermons on important subjects. Selections]
   Principles of revival/Charles G. Finney: compiled and edited by
Louis Gifford Parkhurst
   Selections from the author's Sermons on important subjects.
   Bibliography: p.
   1. Congregationalist churches—Sermons.
2. Sermons. American. 3. Reformed church—sermons
4. Revivals. 5. Conversion.
I. Parkhurst, Louis Gifford, 1946–   .   II. Title.
BX7233.F45S45   1987   243-dc19   87-18433 CIP
ISBN 0-87123-929-9 (pbk.)

CHARLES G. FINNEY was one of America's foremost evangelists. Over half a million people were converted under his ministry in an age that offered neither amplifiers nor mass communications as tools. Harvard Professor Perry Miller affirmed that "Finney led America out of the eighteenth century." As a theologian, he is best known for his *Revival Lectures* and his *Systematic Theology*.

LOUIS GIFFORD PARKHURST, JR., is pastor of First Christian Church of Rochester, Minnesota. He garnered a B.A. and an M.A. from the University of Oklahoma and an M.Div. degree from Princeton Theological Seminary. He is married and the father of two children. This is his tenth volume of the works of Charles G. Finney for Bethany House Publishers.

OTHER BOOKS IN THIS SERIES

OTHER BOOKS BY FINNEY

PREFACE

The following were some of the considerations that influenced me to publish the sermons composing this volume:

I. Garbled extracts which misrepresented certain doctrines had been given to the public by reviewers and those who had taken notes. I therefore thought the public should understand these points, for two reasons. First, those that had confidence in me, and in my views, might adopt these misrepresentations as truth. Second, many individuals might be shut out from ever coming to the truth by prejudices growing out of these misrepresentations.

II. I have read almost nothing else in other literature on these points made in my sermons, nor heard them discussed in a manner satisfactory to me.

III. In preaching as an evangelist, I have found it especially important to discuss these and other topics, and have almost everywhere found many misunderstandings in the minds of the public on most of these points.

IV. As my health has rendered it probable that I shall never be able to labor as an evangelist again, I have thought that it might serve the cause of Christ to publish something on several points that I have found to need discussion and explanation.

Two of these sermons have been published several times in the form of tracts, and I suppose have been extensively read. But as some of my friends have desired to have them in a more permanent form, I have therefore given them a place in the present volume.

This volume contains only a few of the sermons that I have thought I should publish if I get time from my other avocations to commit them to writing. Whether any more of them will ever appear must depend upon the providence and grace of God.*

I make no pretensions to literary merit; simplicity of arrangement and clarity of style have been the two objects at which I have aimed. Whether I have made myself understood will be known when these are read. They have been written in great haste and amidst a multitude of embarrassments and pressing duties. Four to eight hours labor has been all that I have been able to bestow on any of them.

I should have bestowed more labor upon them, and endeavored to have rendered them more acceptable from a literary point of view, had it been possible to spare the time from my other vocations. I have done what I could under the circumstances, and if the Lord can use this volume to do any good, to His name be all the glory.

Charles G. Finney, 1836

---

*Indeed, by the providence and grace of God, Finney's health was somewhat restored, and following these sermons he was able to preach a series of lectures later published as *Lectures on Revivals of Religion*. Finney's sermons continued to be preached and published in "The Oberlin Evangelist" and in books.

Many of these sermons can be found almost exactly as they were preached in the Bethany House Publishers' "Principles Series" for today's readers, which have been edited by L. G. Parkhurst, Jr. God blessed Finney's labors during his lifetime, and his works are empowering many today to live and labor effectively for Christ—to the conversion of many.

CONTENTS

10

INTRODUCTION

On any given Sunday morning, three types of people may be found in church. You would hope to find Christians there who are on fire for the Lord; there would also be professing Christians who publicly proclaim Christ as Lord and Savior without knowing Him or acting out their faith; and there would also be those who do not know God, who are living in bondage to sin. Finney treated professing Christians and unrepentant sinners the same: both need to be born again. Under the anointing of the Holy Spirit, whenever Charles Finney conducted a revival both groups repented and became Christians in deed as well as word.

Principles of Revival is compiled to promote revival that will lead "professing Christians" to total Christian commitment, to holiness of thought and life. These principles will also lead sinners to faith in Jesus Christ as Lord and Savior of their lives as well as help committed Christians lead others to a living faith in Jesus Christ.

The Finney series is being edited to make committed followers of the Lord Jesus Christ. Some people will not become Christians until they hear the gospel presented to them in the way Finney has done. They need particular questions about God, the Bible, and certain Christian teachings answered. (I, for one, could not become a Christian until I learned that my problem was not my "inability" to become a Christian, but my "unwillingness"—a topic Finney deals with here. Yet, I attribute my willingness to the grace of God—as did Finney.) Finney answers many questions that can turn the course of a person's life.

In this book I have edited into short chapters nine messages from *Sermons on Important Subjects*, Finney's first book of published revival sermons, into short chapters. The original work was published in 1836 with twelve sermons printed almost as he had preached them. Finney had been asked repeatedly to publish some authorized versions of the sermons which had brought revival to churches, cities and towns where he had labored. Lay people and preachers wanted to know the topics he had covered and why he had been so successful. They realized that if Finney could preach the gospel and convert his hearers, they could too. Some of his ideas had been misrepresented by his opponents in the church, and some of his sermons had been circulated in incomplete and inaccurate reprints; therefore, Finney finally complied with the many requests.

In *Principles of Revival* I have taken Finney's sermons and divided them into "principles." The book is divided into eight topics covered by Finney's nine sermons (there were two sermons on total depravity). At points I have altered his style and used updated language. Those who have extensively read Finney may be used to his original style and I hope my new approach does not interfere with their reading. I believe that the short, easy-to-read and understand chapters will be helpful for individual and group study.

Finney's teachings have come as a blazing light of truth into the minds of many people, and these have become devoted followers of Christ. However, some may have received so much new knowledge that they have become "puffed up," and have quenched the Holy Spirit and love. Finney remained humble, teachable and loving all of his life. He was never egotistical or legalistic with his vast knowledge of Scripture's teachings. He reached out in love to present the truths God had revealed to him. When we follow this example, the principles in this book will bring revival to our own hearts, revival to our churches and revival to towns and cities all across the globe.

With Love In The Lamb,
L. G. Parkhurst, Jr.

PART 1

Sinners Are Bound to Change Their Own Hearts

"Make you a new heart and a new spirit, for why will ye die?" (Ezekiel 18:31).

PRINCIPLE 1

CONVERSION IS NOT A PHYSICAL CHANGE

When Ezekiel spoke to Israel, they were evidently living as unrepentant sinners, for he commanded, "Make you a new heart and a new spirit, for why will ye die?" The requirement for them to make themselves a new heart and a new spirit was enforced by the weighty penalty of death for disobedience. The death mentioned in the text cannot mean *natural death*, for natural death is common to every man. Nor can it mean *spiritual death*, a state of entire sinfulness; for then it would read, "Why are ye already dead?" *The death spoken of by Ezekiel must mean eternal death*: banishment from God and the glory of His power.

This command to the Israelites is binding upon every unrepentant sinner who hears the gospel. We are required to perform the same duty or suffer the same penalty. We should fully understand and immediately obey the demand.

What does it mean to make a new heart?

A reflecting mind naturally asks the following: What does it mean to make a new heart and a new spirit? Is it reasonable to require this on the risk of suffering eternal death? How is this requirement consistent with the often repeated declarations of the Bible that a new heart is the gift and work of God?

Does God require us to perform this duty without expecting its fulfillment, merely to show us that we are powerless and dependent upon Him to perform it?

Although the Bible was not given to teach us philosophy or psychology, we may rest assured that all its declarations are in accordance with the true philosophy of mind.* In the Bible, words are sometimes used to mean different things in different contexts. We must understand this. For example, the term *spirit* is used in different senses. Sometimes it means a spiritual being or moral agent. In other places *spirit* is used in the sense we often use it casually: speaking of the temper, disposition or character of a person. *Evidently, spirit is used in this sense in Ezekiel's command.*

The term *heart* is also employed in various senses. Sometimes it appears to be synonymous with *soul.* At times it expresses the sense of natural emotions or social affections. At other times *heart* evidently means either the will or the conscience. But sometimes it seems so extensive as to cover all the moral movements of the mind.

The particular senses in which heart and spirit are to be understood in any place may easily be determined by the context in which they stand. Our present business is to understand these words of Ezekiel; for it is in this sense that we are required to make ourselves a new heart and a new spirit.

---

*Finney later wrote concerning this in his *Systematic Theology*: "Theology is so related to psychology that the successful study of one without a knowledge of the other is impossible. Every theological system, and every theological opinion, assumes something as true in psychology. Theology is, to a great extent, the science of mind in its relation to moral law. God is a mind or spirit: all moral agents are in His image. Theology is the doctrine of God, comprehending His existence, attributes, relations, character, works, word, government (providential and moral), and, of course, it must embrace the facts of human nature, and the science of moral agency. All theologians do and must assume the truth of some system of psychology and mental philosophy, and those who exclaim most loudly against metaphysics, no less than others" (*Systematic Theology*: 1851, p. 1.). Finney's revival sermons indicate he had mastered the principles of psychology, but never for the purpose of manipulating his crowds. You will see how carefully Finney distinguishes between the *heart* and the *conscience*, especially in the latter parts of *Principles of Revival* to bring home the truth of the gospel.

God Does Not Alter Our Substance

In our text, *heart* does not mean the fleshly heart, that bodily organ which is the seat of physical life. To make a new *heart* does not mean a new soul—we have one soul, have no need of another, and cannot make another. To make a new *heart* does not mean we are required to create any new faculties of body or mind. We now have all the powers of moral agency we need. We are just as God made us, without need of any alteration in the substance of our soul or body.* We are not required to add to the constitution of our minds or bodies any new principle or desire.

Those who have a new heart have not had any constitutional alteration of their powers. They are the same people they were before, as far as both body and mind are concerned. *The alteration lies in the manner in which they actually employ their moral and physical powers.* A constitutional change, either in body or mind, could destroy personal identity. If this took place in conversion, one who has a new heart would not be the same individual that he was before with regard to his powers of moral agency. Neither would he have the same responsibilities.

A constitutional or physical alteration of a person by the implantation of a new principle in his soul (or diffusing a new desire which is incorporated with and becomes an essential part of his being) would destroy all the virtue of his obedience. It would make obedience to God the mere satisfying of an appetite or emotions in which there would be no real virtue, just as in

---

*Finney recognized that we are fallen and physically depraved from birth. However, this physical depravity is not sinful in itself, but becomes the *occasion* for our eventual and certain moral depravity. The fall is the choice to live on the basis of selfishness (self-centeredness) instead of love (God-centeredness). Finney did not want the sinner to use his physical depravity as an excuse for not changing his disposition or character (heart or spirit). See *Finney's Systematic Theology* (Minneapolis: Bethany House Publishers, 1976, p. 164ff.—from now on referred to as *Systematic Theology*). We must admit, however, that this one sentence in our text, and a few others like it, did cause Finney's critics to rise up against him. For this reason, one of the largest sections of *Principles of Revival* deals with total depravity, beginning with Principle 25. Over the next few years, as a theological professor, Finney began to master the subtleties of theological expression with regard to the historic fall.

eating when we are hungry or drinking when we are thirsty.

The implantation of a principle of holiness in the mind or the creation of a constitutional taste for holiness, if such a thing were possible, would render the perseverance of the saints physically necessary, make falling from grace a natural impossibility, and would thus destroy all the virtue of perseverance.

A Physical Change Would Dispense With the Spirit

A constitutional change would dispense with the need of the Holy Spirit's agency in us after conversion. A re-creation of a person's faculties, the implantation of a holy desire in his mind, would plainly dispense with any other agency on God's part in later life, except that of keeping a person in existence and giving him the power to act. When obeying the laws of his renewed nature or satisfying his new desire, he would obey God by necessity and not by choice.

But we know by experience that the special influences of the Holy Spirit in later life are necessary. Those who have a new heart find that His constant agency is as indispensable to their perseverance in holiness as it was to their conversion.

Also, the idea of a constitutional change is inconsistent with the Bible's warnings against backsliding. For if the mind were changed and a desire for holiness and obedience were implanted in the substance of the soul, it is obvious that to fall from grace would be as naturally impossible as to alter the desires of the body.

A constitutional change is unnecessary in conversion. Some suppose that the motives of the gospel will not move the mind to obedience to God unless something is implanted in the mind that will respond to the outward motive and the gospel as it is presented. In other words, since the motives of the gospel are holy, there must be a holy desire or principle implanted in the substance of the mind before these motives can act at all; for response requires that there be a desire in the mind of the same nature as the outward motive. Those who believe this teach that if the motive is holy, the constitutional desire must be holy; if the motive is sinful, the constitutional desire must be sinful.

But this absurd idea is contrary to experience.

Upon their principles, I would ask how it was possible that holy Adam sinned? Did God or the devil first implant a constitutional sinful desire within him corresponding to the outward motive? How could the holy angels sin? Did God also implant a sinful principle or desire in them? Or were Adam and "the angels that kept not their first estate" originally created with sinful desires similar to those outward motives to sin? If so, they were sinners by creation. Who then is the author of sin and responsible for this wickedness?

It is true that the constitution of the mind must be suited to the nature of the outward motives; for there must be such an adaptation of the mind to the motive and the motive to the mind, so as to produce the desired action of the mind. But it is absurd to say that this constitutional adaptation must be a holy principle, desire or craving after obedience to God.

PRINCIPLE 2

CONVERSION IS A VOLUNTARY CHANGE

All holiness in God, in angels, or in human beings must be *voluntary* or it is not holiness. To call anything that is a part of the mind or body "holy"—to speak of it as holy (unless it is in the figurative sense)—is to talk nonsense.

Holiness is a *virtue*. Holiness is something that is praiseworthy. Therefore, it cannot be a part of the created substance of body or mind. *Holiness consists of voluntary obedience to the principles of eternal righteousness.* The necessary adaptation of the mind to the outward motive lies in the powers of moral agency which every human being possesses. We have understanding to perceive and decide. We have conscience to weigh the nature of moral opposites. We have the power and liberty of choice. Since we, as moral agents, possess these faculties, the motives of the gospel are addressed to these faculties. Plainly, there is a natural tendency in the weighty considerations of the gospel to influence us to obey our Maker.

The Bible often speaks of the *heart* as a fountain from which flows the moral affections and actions of the soul: "Out of the heart proceed evil thoughts, murders, adulteries, fornications, thefts, false witness, blasphemies" (Matthew 15:19). The term *heart* as applied to the mind is figurative, and recognizes an analogy between the heart of the body and the heart of the soul.

The fleshly organ of the body called the *heart* is the seat and

19

fountain of physical life, and its constant action diffuses life through the physical system. *The spiritual heart is the fountain of spiritual life. It is that deep-seated but voluntary preference of the mind which lies behind all its other voluntary affections and emotions, and from which they take their character.* I understand the term *heart* to be used in this sense in the text.

The *spiritual heart* is evidently something over which we have control; something for which we can be blamed, and something we are bound to alter. Now, if we were required to make some constitutional change in the substance of our body or mind, it is evident that the command to change our hearts would be unjust. Since obedience would be impossible, the requirement would be infinite tyranny.

The Supreme Object of the Sinner's Pursuit Must Change

Obviously, we are required to change our *moral character*, our *moral disposition.* We are required to change *that abiding preference of our minds* which prefers sin to holiness and self-satisfaction to the glory of God. A *change of heart*, as the term is used here, is just what we mean by a *change of mind* with regard to the supreme object of pursuit. A *change of heart* is a change of the choice of an *end*, not merely in the choice of a *means.* An individual may change his mind and still prefer different means at different times, but the means are always to accomplish the same end.

A person who proposes to make his own happiness the supreme object of his pursuit may imagine that his highest happiness lies in the possession of worldly goods. In pursuit of this end, he may give himself wholly to the acquisition of wealth while constantly changing his choice of means. He may at one time pursue a business, at another the profession of law, and still later the profession of medicine; however, all these are only changes of mind with regard to the means of accomplishing the same selfish end.

Eventually he may see that his happiness does not consist in material wealth. He may reason that since he is to exist forever, he has a higher interest in the things of eternity than in those of today. Accordingly, he may enlarge his selfish aims, carry forward his interest into eternity, and propose as the supreme object of pursuit the salvation of his soul. He now has an eternal interest instead of a temporal end. But still the goal of his pursuit is his own happiness. His purpose for living is substantially the same: it is only the exercise of selfishness on a wider and extended scale.

Instead of being satisfied with the happiness of today, selfishness aims at securing the bliss of eternity. When we confine our views and desires to the acquisition of worldly goods, we aim at employing the affections, the services, the honors and the wealth of the world. Yet, we can lengthen the cords and strengthen the stakes of our selfishness. We can carry out our aims, desires and exertions toward eternity. We can set ourselves to pray, to read our Bibles, and to become marvelously religious. We could willingly enlist the affections, the powers and the services of all heaven, even those of the eternal God, to achieve our selfish end.

While our views were confined to worldly things, we were satisfied that *people* should be our servants; but now, in the selfish pursuit of our own eternal happiness, we would willingly call on all the attributes of *God* to serve us. But in all this there is no change of heart. We may often have changed our choice of means, but our end has always been the same; our own happiness has been our idol.

A change of heart, then, consists in changing the controlling preference of the mind; choosing a new goal to pursue. The selfish heart prefers self-interest to the glory of God and His kingdom. A new heart chooses the glory of God instead of one's own happiness. In other words, a change of heart is *a change from selfishness to benevolence*, from having a supreme regard for one's own interest to an absorbing and controlling choice of the happiness and glory of God and His kingdom.

We Work for the Ruler We Choose

A change of heart is a change in the choice of a *Supreme Ruler*. Unrepentant sinners demonstrate that they prefer Satan as the ruler of the world; they obey his laws, campaign for his election and are zealous for his interests—even to martyrdom. They sacrifice both body and soul to promote his interests and establish his dominion. A new heart chooses God as supreme governor of the universe.

The world is divided into two great political parties. One party chooses Satan as the god of this world, yields obedience to his laws and is devoted to his interests. Selfishness is the law of his empire. The other party chooses the eternal God for its governor and consecrates all its interests to His service and glory. But changing parties, from Satan's to God's, does not imply an alteration of the parts or powers of body or mind any more than a change of mind with regard to the form or administration of a human government requires a physical change of mind or body. The act is accomplished by choice alone; by a change of heart.

PRINCIPLE 3

CONVERSION IS A CHANGE OF PREFERENCE

We understand some things about the mind by experience. For instance, we know by experience that it is the nature of the mind to be controlled by a deep-seated *disposition* or *preference* for a particular goal. It is not necessary here to enter into the philosophy of this fact, but simply to recognize the fact itself.

When Adam was first created and awoke into being, before he had obeyed or disobeyed his Maker, he could have had no moral character at all. He had exercised no affections, no desires nor made any choices. In this state he was a complete moral agent, and therefore in the image of his Maker. But as yet he had no moral character. Moral character cannot be created, since it attaches to voluntary actions.

Do not understand me to affirm that any considerable time elapsed between the creation of Adam and his possessing a moral character. As soon as he awoke into being and had knowledge of the existence and character of his Maker, the evidence of which doubtless shone all around him, he chose *God* as his Supreme Ruler and voluntarily dedicated all his powers to His service.

Adam's preference for God and His glory and service over his own self-interest and everything else constituted his *disposition* or his *moral character*. He had a perfectly holy heart. Out of this heart, or preference, flowed the pure waters of obedience. All the subordinate movements, affections, choices, purposes of the mind and all the outward actions flowed from this strong governing preference for God and His service. Thus he went forth to dress God's garden and keep it.

Our Preference Directs Our Feelings and Conduct

For a time, Adam's preference was strong enough to insure perfect obedience in all things, since the mind will follow an abiding preference according to the strength and permanence of the preference. For example, the preference that a man may have for home may forbid entertaining any thought of going abroad. His preference for his wife may prevent his consenting to any improper intimacy with other women. The probability, and I may say possibility, of acts of infidelity against his wife depends upon the strength and abiding energy of his choice for her above all other women.

So, while the supreme choice of Adam remained unshaken, its energy gave direction and character to all his feelings and conduct. That which must stamp perfection upon obedience in heaven is the great strength and continuously abiding energy of the saints' preference for God and His service.

The holiness of God flows from this same fountain. It does not consist in the substance of His nature, but in His constant preference of right. His holiness must be voluntary. His preference of right is infinitely strong, so strong and so abiding as never to admit any change or allow conduct inconsistent with it.

Adam was perfectly holy, but not infinitely so. It was possible that he might be changed. We have the melancholy fact revealed on every side of us, which cannot be misunderstood, that an occasion occurred in which Adam actually changed his preference. Satan, as the serpent, presented a very peculiar temptation. It was addressed to the constitutional desires of both soul and body: to the body's desire for food and to the mind's desire for knowledge. These desires were a part of who he was as created by God. They were not in themselves sinful, but their *unlawful indulgence* would be sin. The proposal of the serpent was that Adam should change his mind with regard to the supreme end of his pursuits; and thus change his heart or his whole moral character.

"Yea, hath God said, ye shall not eat of every tree of the garden? and the woman said unto the serpent, we may eat of the fruit of the trees of the garden: but of the fruit of the tree which is in the midst of the garden, God hath said, Ye shall not eat of it, neither shall ye touch it, lest ye die. And the serpent said unto the woman, Ye shall not surely die: for God doth know that in the day ye eat thereof, then your eyes shall be opened, and ye shall be as gods, knowing good and evil" (Genesis 3:1–5).

The Foundation of Adam's Holiness Was His Holy Preference

Now, *the foundation of holiness in Adam*, and that which constituted his holy heart, *was the supreme choice that God should rule*: the supreme preference of God and His glory to his own happiness or interest. Therefore, the aim of the serpent was to affect a change in the *supreme end* or goal of pursuit. The serpent wanted Adam and Eve to pursue their own satisfaction rather than obedience to their Maker, to become gods themselves instead of obeying God, to pursue as a supreme end their own self-satisfaction instead of the glory of God.

When they yielded to this proposal and changed their minds upon this fundamental point, they changed their own hearts (or that controlling preference which was the foundation and fountain of all obedience). They gave up perfectly holy hearts for perfectly sinful ones. There was no constitutional change, no change in the substance of either body or mind. It was not a change in the *powers* of moral agency, but simply in the use of it—in consecrating their energies to a different end.

Suppose God had said to Adam, "Make to you a new heart, for why will you die?" Could Adam have justly answered, "Dost thou think that I can change my own heart?" Might not the Almighty have answered him in words of fire, "Rebel, you have just changed your heart from holiness to sin, now change it back from sin to holiness!"

CONVERSION IS A CHANGE OF GOVERNOR

Suppose an earthly king established a government and proposed as his great goal to produce the greatest happiness possible within his kingdom. To acheive this, he enacted wise and benevolent laws which he too obeyed; laws which were framed so as to result in universal happiness if they were universally obeyed. He required all his subjects to sympathize with him; they all were to be governed by the same principles and pursue the same goal—the promotion of the highest interests of the community.

Further suppose that one individual, after a season of obedience and devotion to the interests of the government and the glory of this king, was induced to stop promoting the public good. He set himself up and said, "I will no longer be governed by the principles of goodwill to the community. I will no longer find my happiness in promoting the public interest. I will aim at promoting my own happiness and glory in my own way, and let the king and his subjects take care of themselves. 'Charity begins at home!' "

Assume that this individual proposed his own happiness and aggrandizement as the supreme object of his pursuit, and did not hesitate to trample upon the laws and encroach upon the rights of his king and his subjects whenever those laws or rights lay in the way of the accomplishment of his designs.

We can easily see that this person has become a rebel. He has changed his *heart*, and consequently his conduct. He has not only separated his interests but opposed the interests of his rightful ruler. From being an obedient subject, he has become a rebel. From obeying his king, he has set up an independent sovereignty. From trying to influence all people to obey the rightful government, from seeking supremely the prosperity and the glory of his king, he has made himself a little king. As Absalom took the men of Israel and kissed them, and thus stole away their hearts, so this man now endeavors to engross the affections, to enlist the sympathies, to command the respect and obedience of all those around him.

What would constitute a change of heart in this rebel toward his ruler? Only if he would go back and change his mind with regard to his supreme objective; prefer the glory of his king and the good of the public to his own separate interest.

God Reigns for Happiness' Sake

This is the case with the sinner. God has established a government and proposed, by the exhibition of His own character, to produce the greatest happiness in the universe. He wisely has enacted laws to promote this, laws to which He conforms His own conduct and to which He requires all His subjects perfectly and undeviatingly to obey.

After a season of obedience, Adam changed his *heart* and set up a kingdom for himself. Every sinner has followed and set up his own interests in opposition to the interests and government of God. Every sinner aims to promote his own private happiness. Self-satisfaction, the minding of the flesh and enmity against God, becomes the law over the general good.

Whenever the preference or goal is changed, we see the need for a corresponding change of conduct. A change of heart, therefore, is to prefer a different *end* or goal; to prefer supremely the glory of God and the public good rather than the promotion of our own interests.

If a person changes sides in politics, you will see him meeting with those who entertain the same views and feelings as he does. He will devise plans and use his influence to elect the candidate with whom he has now chosen to side. He has new political friends on one side, and new political enemies on the other.

So with a sinner; if he changes his heart, you will see Christians become his friends. With Christ as his candidate, he will aim at honoring Him and promoting His interests in all his ways. Before he changed, his motto declared, "Let Satan govern the world." Now the motto of his heart and his life is, "Let Christ rule as King of nations as He is King of saints." His prayer was, "Satan, let thy kingdom come, and let thy will be done." Now his lips cry out, "O Jesus, let thy kingdom come, let thy will be done on earth as it is in heaven."

A Christian Prefers the Interests of God's Kingdom

In proof that the change which I have described constitutes a change of heart (if any proof is necessary), I observe that he who actually prefers the glory of God and the interests of His kingdom to his own selfish interests is a Christian. He who prefers his own selfish interests to the glory of God is an unrepentant sinner.

The fundamental difference between a Christian and a sinner lies in this ruling preference, this fountain, this heart out of which flows the emotions, the affections and actions. As the difference between ruling preferences consists not in the substance of their minds or bodies, but in the voluntary state of mind in which they are, it is just as unphilosophical, absurd, and unnecessary to suppose that a physical or constitutional change has taken place in him who has the new heart as to infer that because a person has changed his politics that his nature is also changed.

Furthermore, this new preference needs only to become deep and energetic enough in its influence to stamp the perfection of heaven upon the whole character. From long-cherished habits of sin and long acting under the dominion of an opposing preference, the newly changed heart is often weak and measurably inefficient. Consequently, the mind often acts inconsistently with its general preference.* Accordingly, God says to Israel, "How weak is thine heart!"

The Christian must allow old habits of thought, feeling, and action to be broken up. His new preference should gain strength, stability, firmness, and permanence to thus take control of the whole person. This process constitutes sanctification.† Every act of obedience to God strengthens this preference and renders future obedience more natural. The perfect control of this preference over all the moral movements of the mind brings a person back to where Adam was previous to the fall, and constitutes perfect holiness.

If a change of heart were physical it would have no moral character. The *change*, to have moral character, must be *voluntary*, a change with regard to the supreme object or goal of pursuit.

Finally, every Christian has passed through the change which I have described. In speaking from experience he can say, "Whereas I once preferred my own separate interests to the glory of my Maker, now I prefer His glory and the interests of His kingdom. I consecrate all my powers to the promotion of them forever."

---

*Charles Finney later wrote that this weakness would be overcome as we develop our faith in Jesus Christ as a present Savior in our daily lives in all the relations that He seeks to have with us. He described these relations in his first edition of his *Systematic Theology*. These relations with Christ have been compiled into a devotional book for daily study under the title *Principles of Union With Christ* (Bethany House Publishers). Finney taught that just as justification is by faith in Jesus Christ alone, so sanctification is by faith in Jesus Christ alone. His first book on sanctification is *Principles of Sanctification* (Bethany House Publishers). His letters on sanctification will be forthcoming as *Principles of Discipleship* (Bethany House Publishers).

†Shortly after the publication of this book of sermons in 1836, Finney and those at Oberlin College began to explore in greater depth the meaning of sanctification in this life. From these studies Finney wrote the lectures and sermons found especially in *Principles of Holiness* and *Principles of Sanctification*. As your study of Finney continues, you will recognize his concern for Christian holiness and sanctification in all his sermons. See especially his sermons on Romans found in *Principles of Liberty* and *Principles of Victory*. The first sermons in *Principles of Devotion* also underscore that a holy life is one of the conditions for God to answer our prayers.

PRINCIPLE 5

CONVERSION IS AN OBLIGATION

The requirement God gives us through Ezekiel is reasonable and equitable. When God tells us to change our hearts *we* are supposed to perform the duty. However, if the change is a physical one, a change substance of the soul, it is beyond our ability, and the command is neither reasonable nor equitable. *To maintain that we are under an obligation to do what we have no power to do is absurd.*

If we are under an obligation to do something and do not do it, we sin. The blameworthiness of sin consists in its being the violation of an obligation. But if we are commanded to do what we have no power to do, then sin is unavoidable: we are forced to sin by our natural inability. But it is unreasonable to make sin consist of anything that is forced upon us by the necessity of nature.

If we are guilty of sin, we are to repent of it, heartily accepting our blame and justifying the requirements of God. But it is impossible for us to blame ourselves for not doing what we never had any power to do.

Suppose God commanded a person to fly. Would the command impose any obligation upon him before he was furnished with wings? Certainly not. But further suppose that upon his failure to obey, God required him to repent of his disobedience, and threatened to send him to hell if he did not heartily accept blame and justify His requirement. He would have to cease reasoning before he could do this. He knows that God never gave him power to fly; therefore, He has no right to require it of him. His natural sense of justice is outraged. He indignantly and conscientiously throws back the requirement into his Maker's face. Repentance in this case is a natural impossibility. He knows that he is not to blame for not flying without wings. However much he may regret his inability to obey the requirement and however great may be his fear of the wrath of God, to blame himself and justify God is a natural impossibility.

God's Demand Evidences Man's Ability

Since God requires people to make themselves a new heart or suffer eternal death, we have the strongest possible evidence that they are able to do it.

To say that God has commanded people to obey Him without telling them they are able is trifling. Their ability is implied in the command. The obligation to change our hearts turns upon the question of our ability; and the question of ability must turn upon the nature of the change itself. If the change is physical, it is clearly beyond the power of man: it is something over which he has no more control than he had over the creation of his soul and body. But if the change is moral, or voluntary, then the requirement of the text is just and reasonable.

We have all the powers of moral agency, to choose between right and wrong. We are not required to alter these powers but to employ them in the service of our Maker. God created them and you can and do use them. He gives you the power to obey or disobey. Sin is to prostitute these powers, which He sustains, to the service of sin and Satan.

Wickedness is a wrong and obstinate choice of sin. Isn't it just as easy to choose right as to choose wrong? The motives for a right choice are infinitely greater than for a wrong one. Could Adam reasonably have objected that he had been unable to change his choice? Could Satan object that he had had no power to change the governing preference of his mind, to prefer the glory of his Maker instead of rebellion against His throne? If

Adam, Satan, or you could object, then wickedness would not exist.

But God only requires you to choose and act reasonably, for it is reasonable to prefer the glory of God and the interests of His immense kingdom to your own private interests. *The glory of God is an infinitely greater good than any other. Therefore, God, you, and all His creatures are obligated to prefer it.*

The motives to choose a right preference are infinitely greater than those to choose a wrong one. Sinners often complain that they are so influenced by motives to do wrong that they cannot resist sin. They often excuse themselves by pleading that the temptation was too strong. Sinner, why is it that you can say you are so easily influenced by motives to sin that you cannot resist them, while you are strong enough to resist the motives that come rolling upon you like a wave of fire to do right and obey your Maker? How inconsistent!

When the Son of God approaches you, gathering motives from heaven, earth and hell, and pours them in a focal blaze upon your mind, how is it that you are strong enough to resist? If you did not exert the whole strength of moral agency to resist, these considerations would change your hearts.

PRINCIPLE 6

CONVERSION IS A GIFT OF GOD

The requirement to "make yourself a new heart" is consistent with the declarations of the Bible that a new heart is the gift and work of God. The Bible ascribes conversion, or a new heart, to four different agencies.

Oftentimes conversion is ascribed to *the Spirit of God*. If you consult the Scriptures, you will find it more frequently ascribed to *the truth*. Examples of this are numerous: "Of his own will begat he us by the word of truth" (James 1:18); "The truth shall make you free" (John 8:32); "Sanctify them through thy truth" (John 17:17); "The law of God is perfect, converting the soul" (Ps. 19:7).

Conversion is sometimes ascribed to *the preacher*, or to the person who presents the truth: "He that winneth souls is wise" (Prov. 11:30); Paul says, "I have begotten you through the gospel" (1 Cor. 4:15); "He that converteth a sinner from the error of his ways shall save a soul from death, and hide a multitude of sins" (James 5:20).

Sometimes conversion is spoken of as the work of *the sinner* himself: "Ye have purified yourselves by obeying the truth" (1 Peter 1:22); "I thought on my ways," says the Psalmist, "and turned unto the Lord" (Ps. 119:59); and again he says, "When thou saidst, Seek ye my face; my heart replied, Thy face, Lord, will I seek" (Ps. 27:8).

Are all these declarations of Scripture consistent with each other? They are all true. They all mean just what they say, but there is no real disagreement among them. There is a sense in which conversion is the work of God, in which it is the effect of truth, in which the preacher brings it about, and in which it is the work of the sinner himself.

The Holy Spirit Is the Primary Agent of Conversion

The actual turning, or change, is the sinner's own act. The agent who induces him is the Spirit of God. The truth is the instrument, or motive, which the Spirit uses to induce him to turn. A secondary agent is the preacher or person who presents the truth.

Imagine yourself standing on the edge of the river by Niagara Falls. As you stand upon the verge of the precipice, you behold a man lost in deep reverie approaching its edge, unconscious of his danger. He walks nearer and nearer, until he actually lifts his feet to take the final step that shall plunge him to destruction. At this moment you lift your warning voice above the roar of the foaming waters, and cry out, "Stop." The voice pierces his ears and breaks the charm that binds him; he turns instantly upon his heel. All pale and aghast he retires, quivering, from the verge of death. He reels, almost swoons with horror, and turns and walks slowly to the public house.

You follow him. His agitated appearance calls many people around him; and upon your arrival he points to you and says, *"That man saved my life."* He ascribes the work to *you*; and certainly there is a sense in which you had saved him. But, on being further questioned, he says, *"Stop!* How that word rings in my ears. Oh, that was to me the word of life." Here he ascribes it to the *word* that aroused him and caused him to turn. But, on conversing still further, he says, "Had I not turned at that instant, I would have been a dead man." Here he speaks of it as *his own act.* But soon, you hear him say, "O, the mercy of God! If *God* had not interposed, I would have been lost."

The Spirit of God Brings Truth to the Sinner's Mind

Now, the only defect in this illustration is this: the only interference on the part of God was a *providential* one. But in the conversion of a sinner, God employs something more than providence; for not only does the providence of God so order that the preacher cry *Stop*, but the Spirit of God forces the truth home upon him with such tremendous power as to induce him to turn.

The Spirit also cries *Stop*. The preacher cries, "Turn, why will ye die?" The Spirit pours the plea home with such power that the sinner turns. In speaking of this change, it is perfectly proper to say that the Spirit turned the sinner just as you would say that the person who had persuaded another to change his mind on the subject of politics had converted him and brought him over. It is also proper to say that the truth converted him. In a case when the political sentiments of a person were changed by a certain argument, we should say that argument brought him over. So also with perfect propriety we may ascribe the change to the living preacher or to him who had presented the motives, just as we would say of a lawyer who had prevailed in his argument with a jury that he had got his case, he had converted the jury.

Just as true is to ascribe conversion to the individual whose heart is changed. It is strictly true that the act is his own act, the turning his own, even though God by the truth has induced him to turn. Still it is strictly true that he has turned himself. Thus it is the work of God and also the sinner's own work. *The Spirit of God, by the truth, influences the sinner to change*, and this is the efficient cause of the change. *But the sinner actually makes a change*, and is therefore himself the author of the change.

Some who read their Bibles fasten their eyes upon those passages which ascribe the work to the Spirit of God, and seem to overlook those which ascribe it to man and speak of the sinner's own act. When they have quoted Scripture to prove it is the work of God, *they seem to think they have proved that in conversion man is passive*, and that conversion can in no sense be the work of man.

Conversion Is Not Entirely God's Work

Someone wrote a tract whose title was *Regeneration Is the Effect of Divine Power*. The writer proves that the work is accomplished by the Spirit of God, and there he stops. Now it would have been just as true, just as philosophical, and just as scriptural had he said that conversion was the work of man. It was easy to prove that it was the work of God in the sense in which I have explained it. *But the writer has told only half the truth.* For while there is a sense in which conversion is the work of God, there is also a sense in which it is the work of man, as we have just seen.

The title of the tract is a stumbling block. *It tells the truth, but it does not tell the whole truth.* The writer, in his zeal to recognize and honor God in this work, left out the fact that a change of heart is the sinner's *own act* and has left the sinner strongly entrenched with his weapons in his rebellious hands, stoutly resisting the claims of his Maker and waiting passively for God to make him a new heart.

Thus you see the consistency between the requirement of the text and the declared fact that God is the author of the new heart. God commands you to do it and expects you to do it. If it is ever to be done, you must do it.

PRINCIPLE 7

SINNERS NEED THE HOLY SPIRIT

Sinners make their own hearts wicked. The sinner's preference for sin is a voluntary act. They make *self-satisfaction* the rule to which they conform all their conduct.

We discover in watching children that they are determined to satisfy themselves. Any effort to thwart the satisfaction of their desires is met with stout resistance. They seem to set their hearts fully to pursue their own happiness no matter what the consequences. Therefore, they will repeatedly make war on their parents and their God whenever they find that the requirements of one of these authorities prohibit the pursuit of self-satisfaction.

Self-satisfaction is a voluntary pursuit. This state of mind was not created in the sinner before birth. It is entirely the result of temptation to selfishness arising out of the circumstances in which the child grows up. The preference for self-interest is allowed by the sinner to grow with his growth, and strengthen with his strength, until his desperately wicked heart bears him onward to the gates of hell.

The necessity of a change of heart is obvious. The Apostle Paul calls the state of mind of unrepentant sinners the "carnal mind"; or as he also rendered it, "the minding of the flesh is enmity against God." The child at first gives up the rein to the bodily desires. God requires him to keep his body under control, to express his soul's wishes in the service of God—to subject and subordinate all his passions to the will of his Maker. But instead of this, he makes the satisfaction of his desires and passions the law of his life.

The apostle speaks of that law in his members as warring against the law of his mind. This state of mind opposes the character and requirements of God. With this heart, the salvation of the sinner is manifestly impossible.

The Spirit Attacks the Sinner's Stubbornness

In the light of this subject, you can see the nature and degree of the sinner's dependence on the Spirit of God. The Spirit's agency is not needed to give him power, but to overcome his voluntary obstinacy. Some people seem to suppose that the Spirit is employed to give the sinner *power*: he is *unable* to obey God without the Spirit's agency.

I am not alarmed when I hear this. I suppose there is a sense in which a person's heart may be better than his head. But I have already shown that a person is under no obligation to do what he has no ability to do; for his obligation is only commensurate with his ability. He cannot blame himself for not having exerted a power that he never possessed. If he believes, therefore, that he has no power to obey his Maker, it is impossible that he should blame himself for not doing it. If he believes that the Spirit's agency is necessary to make him able, he is compelled to maintain that without this superadded agency he is under no obligation to obey God.

Giving the sinner *power* by the aid of the Holy Spirit to obey God is what the Arminians call a *gracious* ability, but this is absurd. What is grace? Grace is undeserved favor, something to which we have no just claim, that which may be withheld without injustice. It is plain that a *gracious ability to do our duty* is absurd. Reason, conscience, common sense and our natural sense of justice dictate that if God requires us to perform any duty or act, He is obligated in justice to give us *power* to obey; He must give us the faculties and strength to perform the act. But if *justice* requires this, why call it a *gracious* ability? Natural ability to do our duty cannot be a *gracious* ability. This confuses the terms grace and justice. The sin of disobedience would then lie not in a person's having broken the law of God, but solely in his not having complied with the strivings of the Spirit.

Accordingly, the definition of sin would not be "a transgression of the law," but would consist in not yielding to the influence of the Holy Spirit. Therefore, before the sinner is aware that the Spirit is giving him power, he is under no obligation to be converted, nor can he blame himself.

How, I would ask, is it possible for him to repent with such views? And how, upon these principles, is he to blame for not having repented and turned to the Lord?

The Spirit Comes with Motives for Obedience

To illustrate both the nature and degree of our dependence on the Spirit, imagine a person bent upon suicide. In the absence of his wife, he loads his pistol and prepares to commit the horrid deed. His little child observes the disorder of his mind and says, "Father, what are you going to do?" "*Be still*," he replies, "I am going to kill myself." The little child weeps, spreads out his little beggar hands, beseeches him to desist, and pours out his little prayers and tears and agonizing entreaties to spare his life. If the eloquence of this child's grief, his prayers and tears, could prevail to change his purpose, he would need no other influence to subdue and change his mind.

But the parent persists, so the child screams to his mother, who flies to the voice of entreaty, and on being told the cause of its anguish, hastens upon the wings of terror to her husband's room and prays that he change his purpose.

By his love for his family, by their love for him, by their dependence upon him—in view of the torn heart and distraction of his wife, by the anguish, the tears and helplessness of his children—by the regard he has for his own soul, by the hope of heaven, by the terrors of hell, by everything tender and persuasive in life, by all that is solemn in the final judgment and terrible in the pains of the second death, she pleads with him, over and over again, not to rush upon his own destruction. If all this can move him, he needs no other and higher influence to change his mind.

But she fails in her efforts. Imagine that she could summon all the angels of God and they also fail to move and melt him by their unearthly eloquence. Some higher power must interfere or the man is lost.

But just as he puts the pistol to his head, the Spirit of God, who knows perfectly the state of the man's mind and understands all the reasons that have led him to this desperate determination, gathers such a world of motive and pours them in such a focused blaze upon his soul that he instantly quails, drops the weapon from his nerveless hand, relinquishes his purpose of death forever, falls upon his knees and gives glory to God.

It was the strength of the man's voluntary purpose of self-destruction alone that made the Spirit's agency at all necessary. If he had yielded to all the motives that had been presented before, and if these had subdued him, no interposition of the Holy Spirit would have been necessary. But it was the wickedness and the obstinacy of the wretch that laid the foundation for the Spirit's involvement.

The Spirit Seeks to Turn the Sinner from Hell

This is the sinner's case. He has set his heart fully to do evil, and if the prayers and tears of friends and of the church of God, the warnings of ministers, the rebukes of Providence, the commands, the pleas, the tears, and groans, and death of God's dear Son; if the offer of heaven, or the threatening of hell could overcome his obstinate preference of sin, the Spirit's agency would not be needed. But because no human or angelic persuasion will cause him to turn, *the Spirit of God must interpose to shake his preference and turn him back from hell.*

The degree of the sinner's dependence upon the Spirit is just the degree of his obstinacy. If the sinner were only slightly inclined to pursue the road to death, then *people* could change him without calling upon God for help; but the strength of his preference for sin makes it necessary that the Spirit should interpose or he is lost. The sinner's dependence upon the Spirit of God, instead of being his excuse, is that which constitutes his guilt. He is all the more guilty, because he *will* not come to Christ with all the motives He has presented him in the gospel apart from the Holy Spirit interceding in his life.

PRINCIPLE 8

SINNERS NEED THE TRUTH

It is very important for us to understand the nature of the Holy Spirit's agency when sinners are converted to Christ. The Holy Spirit does not act by direct physical contact upon the mind, but He uses the truth as a sword to pierce the sinner. *The motives presented in the gospel are the instruments the Holy Spirit uses to change the sinner's heart.*

Some have doubted this, and supposed that it is equivalent to denying the Spirit's agency altogether to maintain that He converts sinners by presenting motives for conversion. Others have denie' the possibility of changing the heart by motives. But the serpent changed Adam's heart by motives. If the old serpent could change a heart from a perfectly holy one to a perfectly sinful one by the power of motives, cannot the infinitely wise God do as much? Truly, to deny this detracts from the wisdom and power of God.

The Scriptures declare that the Spirit converts sinners by the power of motive: "Of his own will begat he us with the word of truth" (James 1:18), is one out of the many express declarations upon this subject. The logic of this is settled by the Bible; we are not at liberty to speculate upon it. We cannot maintain that God interposes and physically changes the sinner's heart irrespective of the truth.

42

The Advocate of Truth

The terms used by our Savior in the promise of the Spirit to reprove the world of sin, of righteousness and of a judgment to come strongly imply the mode of His agency. The Greek term rendered *Comforter* in our translation of the Bible is *Parakletos*. *Parakletos* is the same term which is also rendered *Advocate*. The term in this sense is applied to Jesus Christ: "If any man sin, we have a *Parakletos* [or an *Advocate*] with the Father, even Jesus Christ the righteous" (1 John 2:1). In this passage, Jesus Christ is spoken of as our *Advocate* with God. The *Parakletos* or *Comforter* promised by our Savior is represented as God's *Advocate* to plead His cause with mankind.

The term rendered *reprove* or *convince* in our translation of the Bible is a legal term meaning the summing up of an argument and establishing or demonstrating of the sinner's guilt. Thus the strivings of the Spirit of God with man are not a physical scuffling, but a debate; a strife not of body with body, but of mind with mind, the action and reaction of vehement argumentation.

These remarks will help us answer the question sometimes asked by individuals who seem to be entirely in the dark about whether the Spirit acts directly on the mind or on the truth to convert a sinner.

It is evident from this subject that God never does what He requires the sinner to do in changing the sinner's heart.

Some people are passive, waiting for some mysterious influence, like an electric shock, to change their hearts. But with this attitude they may wait until the day of judgment, because God will never do their duty for them. *Sinners, God requires you to turn, and what He requires of you He will not do for you. It must be your own act. It is not the appropriate work of God to do what He requires of you. Do not wait for Him to do your duty, but do it immediately yourself on threat of eternal death.*

Sinners Must Turn to Receive Grace

This subject also shows that if the sinner is to have a new heart, he must obey the command of the text and make it himself.

But here someone may say, "Is not this taking the work out of God's hands, and robbing Him of the glory?" No. It is the only view of the subject that gives glory to God. Some, in their zeal to magnify the grace of the gospel, entirely overthrow it. They maintain the sinner's *inability* and thereby do away with guilt. Instead of considering him a guilty, voluntary rebel worthy of eternal death, they make him a helpless, unfortunate creature, unable to do what God requires of him. Instead of making his only difficulty an *unwillingness*, they insist upon his *inability*, and thus destroy his guilt, and of course the grace displayed in salvation—for what grace can there be in helping an unfortunate individual? If sinners are unable to obey God, they are innocent in proportion to their *inability*. But if they are *unwilling*, if their *cannot* is actually a *will not*, we have seen that their guilt is in proportion to the strength of their unwillingness, and grace in their salvation must be equal to their guilt.*

It does not detract from the glory of God that the act of turning is the sinner's own. The fact is, *he never does and never will turn unless God induces him to do it*; so that although the act is the sinner's own, the glory belongs to God inasmuch as He caused him to act.† If a person has made up his mind to take his own life, and you, by taking great pains and at great expense, prevail upon him to desist, would you not deserve credit for the influence you exerted in the case? Though changing his

---

*See also *Systematic Theology* for an expanded treatment of two important concepts: "Gracious Ability" (pp. 277–288) and "The Notion of Inability" (pp. 289–299).

†In his later works, Finney was very careful to distinguish between a *causation* and an *influence*. In the physical realm of cause and effect, *cause* is appropriate for the acts of God. However, in the moral realm, in order for people to maintain their personal responsibility and accountability for their actions, the term *influence* is a better term and more appropriate. I believe, if given the opportunity, Finney would have revised his sermon and used the word *influence* here consistently, as he does in his later works. Remember, for Scripture and Finney, salvation is always by grace through faith lest anyone should boast. The sinner must receive the free gift of salvation with the empty hands of faith apart from any human merit or works. None of his return to obedience can atone for the guilt and punishment he deserves for his prior disobedience. Finney will show in latter principles how crucial the atonement of Christ is for the salvation of souls.

mind and relinquishing his purpose of self-destruction was his own act, inasmuch as you were the sole cause of his turning, are you not entitled to just as much praise as if he had not been at all concerned in turning? Might it not in truth be said that you had turned him?

The idea that the Spirit converts sinners by the truth is the only view of the subject that honors either the Spirit or the truth of God.

God Exerts Moral Force Against Sin

The work of conversion is spoken of in the Bible as a work of exceedingly great power. I once heard a clergyman speaking on the great powers of God in conversion—he appeared to view it as a physical alteration of man, as the implantation of a new principle or taste. He asserted that it was a greater exertion of power than that which created the heavens. The reason which he gave was that the creation of the material universe had no opposition, but in the conversion of a soul all the powers of hell oppose God. This is whimsical and ridiculous enough; as if the opposition of hell could place any obstacle in the way of physical Omnipotence!

The Spirit cannot operate upon the mind by direct physical change, for the idea of effectively resisting His physical omnipotence is ridiculous. The same thought applies to those passages that caution us against grieving and quenching the Spirit.

The power which God exerts in the conversion of a soul is *moral* power. *Moral power* is used by a statesman to sway the mind of a senate or by an advocate to move the heart of a jury. "David bowed the heart of all Israel, as the heart of one man" with moral power. Consider the deep-rooted selfishness of the sinner, his long-cherished habits of sin and his multifaceted excuses and refuges of lies. It is a sublime exhibition of wisdom and of moral power to pursue him step by step with truth, to hunt him from his refuges of lies, to constrain him by the force of argument alone, to convince him to yield up his selfishness and dedicate himself to the service of God. This reflects a glory of the truth of God and the agency of the Holy Spirit that both delights and amazes the beholder.

The idea that the Spirit uses motives to change the heart is the only view that gives consistency to the often repeated injunction not to resist the Holy Spirit: that we are not to strive with our Maker.

PRINCIPLE 9

SINNERS NEED SOUND ARGUMENTS

A sinner under the influence of the Spirit of God is just as free as a jury under the arguments of an advocate. Suppose a lawyer in addressing a jury did not expect to change their minds by anything he could say, but waited for an invisible, physical agency to be exerted by the Holy Spirit upon them. Suppose, on the other hand, that the jury thought that in making up their verdict they must be passive and wait for a direct physical force to be exerted upon them. In vain might the lawyer plead, and in vain might the jury listen, for until he pressed his arguments as if he was determined to bow their hearts, and until they made up their minds to decide the question and thus act like rational beings, both his pleading and their listening would be in vain.

So, if a minister goes into a pulpit to preach to sinners, believing that his listeners have no power to obey the truth and that a direct physical influence must be exerted upon them before they *can* believe, he preaches in vain. And if his audience is of the same opinion, they listen in vain. They sin and quietly wait for some invisible hand to be stretched down from heaven to perform some surgical operation, infuse some new principle or implant some constitutional taste, *after* which they suppose they shall be *able* to obey God.

Ministers should labor with sinners as a lawyer does with a jury, and upon the same principles of logic. Sinners should weigh his arguments and make up their minds as though he were under oath and arguing for his life, and give a verdict upon the spot according to the law and evidence.

Why Sinners Will Not Be Saved in Hell

But someone perhaps will ask, "If truth, when seen in all its bearings and relations, is the instrument for converting the sinner, why will he not be converted in hell where it is supposed that all truth will burst upon his mind in its burning reality?" The motive that prevails to turn the convicted rebel to God will be lacking in hell. When the sinner is crowded with conviction, ready to despair, ready to flee and hide himself from the presence of his Maker, he is met by the *offer of reconciliation* which, together with the other motives that are weighing like a mountain upon his mind, sweetly constrains him to yield himself up to God. But in hell the offer of reconciliation will be lacking: the sinner will be in despair, and while in despair it is a moral impossibility for him to turn his heart to God.

Let a person so completely ruin his fortune so as to have no hope of retrieving it. In this state of absolute despair, no motive can reach him to make him put forth an effort. He does not have sufficient motive to attempt it. If his reputation is so completely gone that he has no hope of retrieving it, his despair allows no possibility of reclaiming himself. He is without hope. So in hell, the poor dying sinner will be shut up in despair. His character is gone. His fortune for eternity is lost. There is no offer, no hope of reconciliation, and punishment will only drive him further and further from God for ever and ever.

But, if a right apprehension of the truth presented by the Spirit of God converts a sinner, does it follow that his ignorance is the cause of his sin? No.

If Adam had kept what truth he knew steadily before his mind, he would doubtless have resisted the temptation. But Adam allowed his mind to be diverted from the reasons for obedience. In due time he sinned. When he had fallen, and selfishness began to control him, he was averse to knowing and weighing the reasons for turning back to God. If ever he turned, the Spirit of God must have pressed the subject upon him.

So with every sinner. At first, he sins against what he knows by overlooking the good reasons he has to obey and yielding himself up to the motives for disobedience. If he has ever adopted the selfish principle, his ignorance becomes willful and sinful. Unless the Spirit of God induces him, he *will* not see. He knows enough truth to leave him without excuse, but he will not *consider* it and let it have its effect upon him.

The Sinner Hates God as He Is

But the objector may still ask, "Is it not true, after all, if a full knowledge of truth is all that is necessary to subdue the sinner, that he only needs to know the true character of God to love Him, and that his enmity against God arises out of his false notions of Him? Is it not a *false* rather than the *true* character of God that he hates?" No.

He hates the true character of God. He hates God for what He *is*, and not for what he is not. The sinner's character is selfishness: God's character is benevolence. These are eternal opposites. The sinner hates God because God is opposed to his selfishness. While a person remains selfish, it is absurd to say that he is reconciled to the true character of God.

But is his ignorance the cause of his selfishness? No, for he knows better than to be selfish. It is true he does not *consider* the unreasonableness of selfishness unless compelled by the Holy Spirit. The work of the Holy Spirit is not merely giving *instruction*, but compelling people to *consider* truths which he already knows: to think upon his ways and turn to the Lord. He brings to the sinner's *attention* those motives which he hates to consider and feel the weight of. It is almost certain that if all the motives to obedience had been clearly before the mind of Adam or any other sinner, and had the mind duly considered them *at the time*, they would not have sinned. But the fact is, sinners do not set what truth they know before their minds. They divert their attention and rush on into hell.

The Source of Ignorance

Will anyone still reply that it is not the Spirit's business to remove the *ignorance* caused by the sinner's willful rejection of light? What does thinking about the truth do but bring the sinner to a more just knowledge of himself, of God and of his duty, and thus, by force of truth constrain him to yield? The Apostle Paul views the subject in this light. In speaking of sinners, he says, "Having their understanding darkened, being alienated from the life of God through the *ignorance* that is in them, because of the blindness of the heart."

Indeed, pressing the truth upon the sinner induces him to turn. But it is not true that he is ignorant of these truths. He knows he must die, that he is a sinner, that God is right and he is wrong, that there is a heaven and a hell, but as the prophet says, "They will not see . . . My people will not *consider*." The Holy Spirit employs His agency not mainly to *instruct*, but to lead the sinner to *think upon his ways*, and ultimately to bring him to repentance.

PRINCIPLE 10

SINNERS NEED CONVICTION OF SIN

Some might ask if my view is inconsistent with the mystery of which Christ speaks when He says, "The wind bloweth where it listeth, thou hearest the sound thereof, but canst not tell whence it cometh nor whither it goeth; so is every one that is born of the Spirit"? I answer, *no.*

The objector argues, "I have considered the subject of a new heart a very mysterious one, but you make it plain. How is this? Does not Christ in the quoted text represent it as mysterious?" I would ask where does Christ represent the mystery of the new birth as beyond understanding? Not in the effects which the Spirit produces, for they are matters of experience and observation. Not in the instrumentality used, for this is often revealed in the Bible.

The mystery lies in the manner of the Spirit's communicating with mind. How disembodied spirits communicate with each other we are unable to say—or how they can communicate with one that wears a body we do not know. We do know that we communicate with each other through the medium of our bodily senses.

"The Truth Was Kept Before His Mind"

Every Christian knows that in some way the truth was kept before his mind, made to bear and press upon him and hedge

51

him in until he was constrained to yield. These are matters of experience, but in what particular manner the Holy Spirit did this is just as mysterious as millions of other facts which we daily witness but cannot explain.

But some will ask why the sinner needs the Spirit of God if he is able to convert himself. Suppose a person owed you one hundred dollars and was abundantly able but wholly unwilling to pay you. You sue him, giving him a motive that will constrain him to pay his debts. Just so with the sinner. *He is able to do his duty, but is unwilling; therefore, the Spirit of God supplies him with motives to make him willing.*

When sinners have inquired what they must do to be saved, it has been common for believers to substitute something for the scriptural demand to change their heart. They have told them to pray that God would change their heart using words like, "You must remember that you are dependent on God for a new heart. Do not attempt to do anything in your own strength—attend to your Bible, use the means of grace, call upon God to change your heart and wait patiently for the answer."

Praying for a New Heart Is Not Sufficient

Sinners should not content themselves with praying for a new heart. A few years ago, a lawyer under deep conviction of sin came to me to inquire what he should do to be saved. When he was in college he, along with two others, had been deeply anxious for their souls. He said that they called on the president and asked him what they should do. His directions were, in substance, that they should read their Bibles, keep clear of vain company, use the means of grace and pray for a new heart. Before long they would either be converted or would give up reading their Bibles and using the means for their salvation.

He replied that it turned out as the president had told them: they soon gave up reading their Bibles and using the means of grace. He said that the directions relieved his mind, and that the more he prayed and used the means the less he felt distressed. He thought he was doing his duty; the more he read his Bible and prayed, the more acceptable he thought himself to God and the more likely to be converted. The more diligent he was in using means, the more self-complacent he became. Thus he waited for God to change his heart until his convictions had entirely worn away, and with a burst of grief he added, "Thus it turned out with all of us. The other two are confirmed drunkards, and I have well nigh ruined myself by drink. Now if there is any hope in my case, tell me what I shall do to be saved." I told him to repent, and pressed him to action. He yielded himself up to God to all appearance.

The result of the directions given by the president was strictly philosophical. The advice was just what would please the devil. It answered his purpose infinitely better than to have told them to abandon all thoughts of religion at once, for this would have shocked and frightened them; and anxious as they were, they would have turned with abhorrence from such advice. But giving them this sanctimonious method of praying and waiting for God to do *what He required of them* was soothing to their consciences.

The president substituted another requirement for the command of God, fostered the young men's spirit of delay and confirmed them in self-righteousness. It was perfectly natural and reasonable if they fulfilled their *duty* to suppose that they were growing better, that the more diligent they were in their unrepentant endeavors, the more they might rely upon God's converting them. Therefore, the longer they proceeded like this, the less they would understand themselves, their danger and their deserved punishment, and the more certainly would they grieve away the Spirit of God.

The Sinner Must Not Wait for God to Act

Sinner! Do not wait and pray for God to change your heart. You should at once put forth the effort and change the governing preference of your mind.

But some may ask, "Can the carnal mind, which is enmity against God, change itself?" I have already said that this text in the original reads: "The minding of the flesh is enmity against God." This *minding of the flesh* is *a choice or preference to satisfy the flesh*. It is absurd to say that a choice can change itself; but it is not absurd to say that the agent who exercises choice can change it.

Sinner! Your obligation to love God is equal to the excellence of His character, and your guilt in not obeying Him is equal to your obligation: infinite. You cannot, therefore, for a moment defer obedience to the commandment in the text without deserving eternal damnation.

PRINCIPLE 11

SINNERS NEED TO MAKE A DECISION

If sinners are converted, it is reasonable to expect them to be converted while a preacher holds up the truth in all its blaze before their minds.

An opposing idea has prevailed in the church that sinners must have a protracted season of conviction. Sudden conversions are of a suspicious character. But certainly "this persuasion cometh not from God." We do not read in the Bible of cases of lengthy conviction. Peter was not afraid that his listeners had not conviction enough on the day of Pentecost. He did not tell them to pray and labor for a more impressive sense of their guilt and then wait for the Spirit of God to change their hearts. He urged their immediate duty upon them. If he had allowed them to escape, to go from under his voice while yet in their sins, it is probable that hundreds—if not thousands—of them would not have been converted at all.

It is as reasonable to expect the sinner to turn, if he turns at all, while listening to the arguments of the preacher as it is to expect a juror to be convinced under the arguments of the lawyer. The advocate does not act upon the preposterous supposition that it is more likely that the jury will be convinced and make up their verdict in his favor when they have retired and calmly considered the subject. His object is to thoroughly convince, to so completely imbue their minds with the subject, as to get their intellect, conscience and heart to embrace his views. This is wise, and in this respect "the children of this world are in their generation wiser than the children of light."

If you go away without changing your heart, it is most probable that your mind will be diverted. You will forget many things that you have heard. The motivations that now press upon you may be abstracted from your mind. You will lose the clear view of the subject that you now have. You may grieve the Holy Spirit, defer repentance and push your unbroken footsteps to the gates of hell.

It is important to present these truths to induce the sinner to change his heart.

The Gospel Is Meant to Disarm the Sinner

Few more devious ideas have been advanced than that there is no logical connection between means and end in the conversion of sinners; that there is no natural adaptedness in the motives of the gospel to annihilate the sinner's selfishness and lead him to submit to God. This idea is a part of the scheme of physical depravity. It considers regeneration a change in the substance of the mind by the Spirit of God, irrespective of truth. If the work is a physical creation, performed by the direct physical power of the Holy Spirit, then certainly it is accomplished by *no means* whatever. But this is so far from truth that no sinner ever was or ever will be converted except by means wisely and logically adapted to this end.

The Spirit selects considerations, under certain circumstances, that are naturally calculated to disarm the sinner; to strip him of his excuses, answer his cavils, humble his pride and break his heart. The preacher should therefore acquaint himself with the sinner's refuges of lies, and take into consideration his whole history, including his present views and state of mind. He should wisely select a subject, skillfully arrange it, simply and yet powerfully present it so as to engage the sinner's attention and then lay himself out to the utmost to bring the sinner to yield upon the spot. He who deals with souls should study well the laws of mind (logic), and carefully and prayerfully adapt his manner to the state, circumstances, views and feelings in which he may find the sinner at the time. He should present in a manner that shall have the greatest *natural tendency* to subdue the rebel at once.

If people would act as wisely and as logically in attempting to make others Christians as they do in attempting to sway them upon other subjects, if they would adapt their subject to the state of mind, conform "the action in the word and the word to the action" and press their subject with as much skill and warmth and perseverance as lawyers and statesmen do their speeches; the result would be the conversion of hundreds of thousands, and converts would be added to the Lord "like drops of the morning dew."

If every church and pastor were right upon this subject, were they imbued with a right spirit, they would "go forth with tears, bearing precious seed, they would soon reap the harvest of the whole earth, and return bearing their sheaves with them."

God Converts Souls

The importance of understanding that God converts souls by motives is inconceivably great. Those who do not *practice* this truth are more likely to hinder than to aid the Spirit in His work. Some have denied it in theory, but have happily admitted it in practice. They have prayed and preached and talked as if they expected the Holy Spirit to convert sinners by the truth. In such cases, notwithstanding their theory, their practice was blessed by God.

But a lack of attention to this truth in practice caused much ruinous error in revivals and in dealing with anxious souls. Much of the preaching, conversation, and exhortation has been irrelevant, perplexing, and mystical. Counselors have failed to demand response to the truth while the sinner was still deeply interested. Spiritual guides withheld particular truths which, above all others, sinners needed to know. Sinners have been perplexed and confounded by abstract doctrines (such as inability, physical regeneration, and constitutional depravity), metaphysical subtleties and absurd exhibitions of the sovereignty of God, until the agonized mind, discouraged and mad from contradiction and absurdity, dismissed salvation as altogether incomprehensible, and postponed the performance of duty as impossible.

You can see the importance of pressing the sinner with every argument and every consideration that can have any weight.

If you remain in sin while the subject is before you, will you yield? Keeping yourself away from the motivations to believe by neglecting church and the Bible or refusing to make up your mind and yield will prove fatal to your soul. "I beseech you, by the mercies of God, that you *at this time* render your body and soul, a living sacrifice to God, which is your reasonable service." Let the truth take hold upon your conscience, throw down your rebellious weapons, give up your refuges of lies and fix your mind steadfastly upon the motivations to accept the offer of reconciliation while it lies before you. Another moment's delay and it may be too late forever. The Spirit of God may depart from you, the offer of life may be made no more, and this final offer of mercy may close up your account and seal you over to all the horrors of eternal death. Hear, then, O sinner, I beseech you to obey the word of the Lord—"Make you a new heart and a new spirit, for why will ye die?"

PART 2

How to Change
Your Heart

*"Make you a new heart and a new spirit, for
why will ye die?" (Ezekiel 18:31).*

PRINCIPLE 12

GREAT EXCITEMENT IS NOT NECESSARY

In Part One, I discussed the meaning of the command in the text, its reasonableness and its consistency with those passages which declare a new heart to be the gift and work of God. I endeavored to show that the *heart* in the text does not mean that bodily organ which is the seat of physical life. Nor does it mean a new soul. We are not required to create any new faculties of body or mind nor alter our constitutional powers, propensities or the susceptibilities of our nature. We are not required to implant any new principle or taste in the substance of either body or mind.

I also endeavored to show that a change of heart is not done to a sinner but by him. The change is not *physical* but *moral*: it is the sinner's own act. It is a change of mind or disposition with regard to the supreme object of pursuit: a change in the *end* at which a person aims, and not merely a change in the *means* of obtaining his goal. There must be a change in the governing preference of the mind. The sinner must change by preferring the glory of God and the interests of His kingdom to his own happiness and to everything else. It is a change from a state of selfishness, in which a person prefers his own interest above everything else, to that disinterested benevolence which prefers God's happiness and glory to his own private happiness.

I endeavored to show how reasonable this duty is by showing

the sinner's ability and need for a new heart. And also, I showed that there is no inconsistency with those passages which declare that a new heart is the gift and work of God.*

How to Change Your Heart

When anxious sinners are commanded to change their hearts and are convinced that it is their duty to do so, they often wish to know how. This is especially true when they know the dreadful consequences of neglecting to obey. They anxiously ask, "How shall I do it? By what process of thought or feeling is this great change to be wrought in my mind?" The following principles will help you out of this dilemma; clearing up what seems to be so mysterious.

You cannot change your heart by exciting your feelings. Sinners are prone to suppose that great fears, terrors, horrors of conscience and the utmost excitement that the mind is capable of bearing must necessarily precede a change of heart. They are led to this by the fact that such feelings do often precede this change. But sinners should understand that this excitement, these fears, alarms and horrors are just the result of ignorance or obstinacy, and sometimes both. Sinners will often avoid changing their hearts until the Spirit of God has driven them to extremity, until the thunders of Sinai have been rolled in their ears and the lurid fires of hell have flashed in their faces. This is not part of making a new heart, but is the result of resistance to the performance of the duty. These terrors are not essential, but are rather an embarrassment and hindrance.

It is illogical to suppose that because *some* sinners have had

_____

*By "disinterested benevolence" Finney does not mean "uninterested benevolence" or benevolence that is uninterested in the methods, means, results, or goals of love and its actions. "Disinterested benevolence" is benevolence or active love for the sake of the object or objects (God and others), because of their own intrinsic value, the worth they have in themselves, without selfish regard or a concern for what return might come to me for my loving actions. "Disinterested benevolence" is *agape* love; love that is impartial, unbiased, free from self-interest or concern for reward or recognition. "Disinterested benevolence" is true virtue, and is further described in Finney's *Principles of Love.*

horrors of conscience before they have yielded to God that, therefore, these fears of hell are *necessary*. You would not maintain that all your children must be threatened with the uplifted rod and thus be thrown into great consternation before they *can* obey simply because one of your children had been obstinate and refused obedience until you had been driven to extremities.

If you are willing to do your duty, fears and great excitement of mind are wholly unnecessary. God has no delight in them for their own sake, and never causes them unless driven to necessity by persistent obstinacy. God often sees it unwise to produce these great terrors and would sooner let the sinner go to hell without them.

Emotions Do Not Change the Heart

You cannot change your heart by an attempt to force yourself into a certain state of emotion. When sinners are called upon to repent and give their hearts to God, it is common for them to undertake this duty by making an effort to *feel emotions* of love, repentance and faith. They seem to think that religion consists of excited feelings called into existence by a direct effort of the will. They spend much time in prayer for certain feelings, and make many agonizing efforts. But these emotions cannot be brought into existence by a *direct effort to feel*. The will has no *direct* influence over the emotions.

Emotions are dependent upon *thought*. They arise spontaneously when the mind is intensely occupied. Thought is under the direct control of the will. We can direct our *attention* and meditations to any subject, and the corresponding emotions will spontaneously arise. If a hated subject is under consideration, emotions of hatred arise. If an object of terror, of grief or of joy occupies the thoughts, the corresponding emotions will naturally arise with a strength corresponding to the intensity of our thoughts upon that subject. Thus our feelings are only *indirectly* under the control of the will. They are sinful or holy only as they are indirectly brought into existence by the will.

People often complain that they cannot control their feelings. They form overwhelming attachments and become offended—their anger arises—but they profess that they cannot help it. It is the preoccupation of the mind which determines the emotions they complain will exist naturally. If an emotion is not approved by our conscience, the corresponding subject must be dismissed from our thoughts and our attention must be directed to some other subject. Offenses must be dismissed and our thoughts occupied with other considerations, or emotions of hatred will continue to fester in our minds. "If a man look on a woman, to lust after her, he has committed adultery with her already in his heart." He is responsible for the feelings after allowing such a subject to occupy his thoughts.

PRINCIPLE 13

MAINTAIN RIGHT FEELINGS

Freedom of choice is indispensable to moral character. If an action is worthy of praise or blame, our universal conviction is that it must be free. Suppose you see a stone fall from a building upon which people are working and a man is killed. If you discover it was an accident, you blame no one for murder. But if you learn that the stone was maliciously thrown upon the head of the man by one of the workmen, you could not resist the conviction that it was murder. So, if God or any other being should push a dagger into your hand and force you to stab your neighbor, the universal conscience would not condemn you, but condemn the one who forced you to do this deed.

Any *moral action, thought or feeling* must be directly or indirectly under the control of the will. If a person voluntarily places himself in circumstances which call wicked emotions into exercise, he is entirely responsible for them. If he places himself in circumstances where virtuous emotions are called forth, he is praiseworthy in the exercise of them precisely in proportion to his free choice to bring his mind into circumstances to cause their existence.

Love Is a Choice for God and His Kingdom

Love, repentance and faith may exist in the mind as either *volition* or *emotion*. Love as *volition* is a simple preference of the mind for God and His kingdom over everything else. This preference may, and often does, exist in the mind so entirely separate from what is termed emotion or feeling that we may be entirely insensible to its existence. But even though its existence may not be a matter of *consciousness*, its *influence* over our conduct will evidence its existence.

In a similar manner, a man engaged in business away from home exercises no felt love for his family, but his *preference* remains the mainspring that directs his movements in his business. He seeks to make provision for his family. His conduct is modified and governed by this abiding, though insensible, preference for them. At the same time, his thoughts are so entirely occupied with other things that no *emotion* or *feeling* of affection exists in his mind.

When the business of his day is past, and other things cease to demand his attention, this preference of home, wife and family comes forth and directs his thoughts. No sooner are they brought before his mind than the corresponding father and husband emotions awake and enkindle in his heart.

So the Christian, while his thoughts are intensely occupied with business or study he may sense no *emotions* of love to God. But as a *Christian*, his preference for God will influence all his conduct. He will neither act nor feel like an ungodly person under similar circumstances. He will not curse, swear or get drunk. He will not cheat, lie or act as if under the dominion of unmingled selfishness. His preference for God will govern his conduct so that while he has no emotional enjoyment of the presence of God, he is indirectly influenced in all his ways by a regard for His glory. When the bustle of business is past, his abiding preference for God naturally directs his thoughts to Him and to the things of His kingdom; corresponding emotions will arise and warm feelings of love will enkindle and restore his soul. He understands the declaration of the Psalmist when he says, "While I mused the fire burned."

Repentance Is an Act of the Will

Repentance properly signifies a change of mind with regard to the nature of sin and does not include the idea of sorrow. It is simply an act of will: rejecting sin and choosing holiness. This is its form as *volition*. When existing as an *emotion*, it sometimes rises into a strong abhorrence of sin and love of holiness. It often melts away into relentings of heart, gushings of sorrow and the strong feelings of self-abhorrence in view of our own sins.

Faith may also exist simply as a settled conviction of the truths of revelation, and will have greater or less influence according to the strength of this persuasion. It is not evangelical faith, however, unless this persuasion is accompanied by the actions of the will.

Demons and wicked people may have a strong conviction of the truth, so strong that they tremble, but they may still hate the truth. *When the conviction of gospel truth is accompanied with the consent of the will, it is evangelical faith*; in proportion to its strength it will influence conduct. This is faith existing as *volition*. When the objects of faith, revealed in the gospel, are the subjects of intense thought, faith rises into *emotion*. It becomes confidence so sensible as to calm all the anxieties and fears of the soul.

Not All Emotions Have Moral Character

Emotions of love or hatred to God that are not directly or indirectly produced by the will have no moral character. A Christian under circumstances of strong temptation may feel emotions of opposition to God rankling his mind. If these emotions are forced upon him by Satan against his will, he is not responsible for them. If he diverts his attention, if he flees from the scene of temptation, if he resists and represses these emotions, he has not sinned. Such emotions are usually brought to exist in the mind of a Christian by some false view of the character or government of God. Emotions of love for God may exist in the mind that are purely selfish; they may arise out of a persuasion that God has a particular regard for us. If this love is not founded upon a preference for God as He really is, it is not virtuous love. In this case, the will may indirectly produce selfish emotions from the selfish preference of the heart.

To change your heart, as I have said repeatedly, is to change the governing preference of your mind. Your *will* should reject sin and prefer God and obedience to Him over everything else. The question is, then, how is your will to be thus influenced? Until your will is right, it is vain to expect emotions of true love to God and of repentance and faith. These feelings which you are seeking and into which you are trying to force yourself need not be expected until your will is bowed, until the ruling preference of your mind is changed.

PRINCIPLE 14

KNOW WHAT MOTIVATES YOU

There are three classes of motives that influence the will. *First*, those that are purely *selfish*. Selfishness is the preference of personal interest and happiness, rather than God and His glory. Whenever the will chooses directly or indirectly under the influence of selfishness, the choice is sinful. All selfishness is sin.

The *second* class of motives are those that arise from *self-love*. Self-love is a constitutional dread of misery and love of happiness. God created us to love ourselves without being selfish. Whenever the will is influenced purely by self-love, its decisions either have no moral character at all or they are wholly sinful. The constitutional desire of happiness and dread of misery is not in itself sinful. The consent of the will to lawfully gratify this love is not sinful. But, when the will consents, as in the case of Adam and Eve, to a prohibited indulgence, then self-love becomes sinful.

A *third* class of motives that influences the will are connected with *conscience*. Conscience is the judgment which the mind forms of the moral qualities of actions. When the will is decided by the voice of conscience or a regard to *right*, its decisions are virtuous. Only when the mind chooses at the bidding of principle are its decisions according to the law of God.

The Bible Appeals to *Self-Love* and *Conscience*

The Bible never appeals to *selfishness* as a motive to influence our decisions or actions. It often appeals to *self-love*, the hopes and fears of people, because self-love is not in itself sinful. When the Bible appeals to hopes and fears, then even the minds of selfish people are prepared for the enlightened and powerful urgings of conscience.

The constitutional principle of self-love does not ultimately determine the mind's choice of obedience to God. When, under the combined influence of hope, fear and conscience, the mind has been led to the full consideration of the claims of God, to admit and cherish the influences of the Holy Spirit so that it becomes enlightened and is led to see what duty is, then the mind is ripe for a decision. Then conscience has a firm footing: the opportunity to exert its greatest power upon the will.

If the will decides virtuously, the *attention* is not occupied with hopes or fears or with those considerations that excite them; but it must be occupied either with the reasonableness, fitness and propriety of its Maker's claims, or with the hatefulness of sin or with the stability of His truth. The decision of the will is not made mainly because you hope to be saved or fear to be damned, but because to act thus is right: to obey God, to serve Him, to honor Him and promote His glory is reasonable and right and just. This is a virtuous decision. This is a change of heart.

The offer of pardon and acceptance has a powerful influence by fully demonstrating the unreasonableness of rebellion against our God. While in despair, the sinner would rather flee than submit. But the offer of reconciliation annihilates despair and gives conscience its utmost power.

You cannot change your heart by listening to your feelings. It is common for people to turn their thoughts upon themselves to see whether they possess the proper feelings: whether they have conviction enough or the emotions which they suppose precede a change of heart. When they divert their mind from the motives to change their heart and fix their attention upon their present mental state, they inevitably lose what feelings they had, rendering a change impossible for the present.

Emotions Arise From the Focus of Thought

Our feelings have a felt existence in the mind. But if they become the subject of *attention*, they cease to exist. While our thoughts are engaged with things outside ourselves, with our past sins, with the character or requirements of God, with the love or sufferings of the Savior or with any other subjects, corresponding emotions will exist in our minds. But, if we turn our attention from all these to our feelings and attempt to examine them, then there is no longer anything before the mind to make us feel: our emotions cease.

While a person stares at an object, its image is painted on the retina of his eye. While he continues to look at the object, the image will remain there and the corresponding impression will be seen in his mind. But if he looks away, the image changes. Should he direct his attention to the mental impression instead of the object that caused it, the impression would also be effaced from his mind.

Therefore, instead of waiting for certain feelings, or making your present state of mind the subject of attention, please distinguish your thoughts from your present emotions and give your undivided attention to some of the reasons for changing your heart.

Remember the objective is not *directly* to create specific emotions, but, by leading your mind to an understanding of your obligations, to induce you to yield to principle and choose what is right. If you will give me your attention, I will give you ideas to consider which are calculated to induce the state of mind which allows a change of heart.

Thoughts to Promote Conversion

Fix your mind upon the unreasonableness and hatefulness of selfishness. Selfishness is the pursuit of one's own happiness as a supreme good. This is inconsistent with the glory of God and the highest happiness of His kingdom. You must realize that you have always, directly or indirectly, aimed at promoting your own happiness in everything, that God's glory and happiness has not been the leading motive of your life and that you have served only yourself.

Your happiness is of trivial importance compared with the happiness and glory of God and the interests of His immense kingdom. To pursue it as a supreme good is to prefer an infinitely lesser good simply because it is *your own*. Is this virtue? Public spirit? Benevolence? Is this loving God supremely, or your neighbor as yourself? No. It is exalting your own happiness in the place of God. It is placing yourself as the center of the universe, and attempting to cause God and all His creatures to revolve around you as your satellites.

Successfully pushing your selfish aims would ruin the universe. A selfish being can never be happy until his selfishness is fully satisfied. Therefore, only one selfish being can be fully satisfied. Selfishness aims at appropriating all good to self. Give a selfish person a county and he will covet a state. Give him a state and he will long for the nation. The nation in hand, he will not rest without the world. Give him the world and he is wretched unless he can rule the universe. He would not be happy unless God himself were prostrate at his feet. His ambition could not be satisfied; his heart could not rest. If, then, you could succeed in your selfish aims, your success would ruin everybody else.

Is this right? If you could ascend the throne of Jehovah, wield the scepter of universal government, appropriate to yourself the honor and the wealth of the entire universe and receive the homage and the obedience of God and all His creatures, the very elements of your nature would still be outraged. The conscience would condemn you, the very laws of your moral constitution would mutiny. Self-accusation and reproach would fight in your heart. You would be forced to abhor yourself.

PRINCIPLE 15

REJECT YOUR SELFISHNESS

If you are selfish, all moral beings should hate you. Furthermore, it is impossible for you, a moral being, to be happy while knowing you are *deservedly* despised. The love of acceptance is a law of our nature: it is laid in the very constitution of the mind by the Hand that formed us. We would need to alter the very structure of our being to love ourselves when we are deservedly hated. It is foolish for you to expect to be happy in the exercise of selfishness. God, angels and saints, wicked men, devils and the entire universe of moral beings must be conscientiously opposed to you while you sustain a selfish character—while your conscience continually gives forth the verdict that you deserve their hatred and pronounces you unfit for anything other than hell.

If you are selfish, look at your guilt. If your example should have its natural influence and not be counteracted by God, it would leaven the whole lump. If all your acquaintances copied your example, and their acquaintances copied theirs, and so on, you can easily see that your influence would soon destroy all benevolence and introduce universal rebellion against God. You have never obeyed God, and all your efforts have been against His government. If God were not constantly wakeful in counteracting the sinner's influence, His government would have been demolished long ago, and virtue and obedience and love to God and man would have been banished from the world.

Selfishness Establishes Satan's Dominion

Your selfishness tends to establish forever the dominion of Satan over others. It is the law of Satan's empire. Have you perfectly obeyed it? Since example preaches louder than precept, have you used the most powerful means possible to induce all mankind to obey the devil? But God has virtuous subjects on earth; no thanks to you if all people are not in league with hell and by their example, at least; shouting forth, "Oh Satan, live forever!"

If you are selfish you have done nothing to save mankind. Your whole life has had a natural tendency to destroy them. Your neglect and contempt of God have exerted the strongest influence within your power to lead them in the way to death. You have done nothing to save yourself, and by neglecting your own soul you have virtually said to your family and friends, "Leave religion alone. Who is the Lord that we should obey Him, or what profit would we have should we pray unto Him?"

Now look at the guilt of selfishness. The guilt of any action is equal to the evils which it has a natural tendency to produce. Your selfishness has the natural tendency to ruin the world, to destroy God's government, to establish Satan's and to people hell with all mankind.

Loving God Is the Reasonable Choice

Turn your attention now to the reasonableness and utility of benevolence, good will. Benevolence to God is preferring His happiness and glory to all other good. Benevolence to others is the exercise of this same regard to them and a desire for their happiness as we have for our own. Benevolence to God is right because His happiness and glory are infinitely the greatest good in the universe. He prefers His own happiness and glory to everything else, not because they are *His own*, but because *they constitute the greatest good*. All beings, when compared with Him, are less than nothing. His capacity for enjoying happiness or enduring pain is infinite, not only in duration but in degree. If all the creatures in the universe were completely happy or perfectly miserable through all eternity, their happiness or misery would only be finite. But God's happiness is not only endless in duration but infinite in degree. It is as much more valuable than that of all the happiness of His creatures as infinite exceeds finite. Therefore, is it not right that all His creatures should value His happiness and glory infinitely above their own? Is it not right that He should do this because it is an infinitely greater good?

Does not the eternal law of justice demand that God should regard His own happiness according to its real value? Has He any right to prefer the happiness of His creatures above His own? Justice requires that He regard everything in the universe according to its relative importance. Should He not require all His intelligent creatures to do the same? Therefore, to have a supreme regard for your own happiness, to value it more than you do the happiness and glory of God is to trample upon the eternal principles of justice which God is bound to maintain. You would array yourself in the attitude of open and outrageous war against God, against the universe, against the principles of your own nature and against whatever is lovely and of good report.

To love your neighbor as yourself is agreeable to the immutable law of right. You should regard the happiness of all mankind as well as your neighbor's according to its real value. The relative importance of each individual's happiness and the happiness f the aggregate whole is more valuable than yours. To refuse to do this is to sin against God and to declare war against all men.

Benevolence Is the Choice for Happiness

Look also at the *utility* of benevolence. The mind is so constituted that benevolent affections are the source of happiness, and malevolent ones the source of misery. God's happiness consists in His benevolence. Wherever there is untainted benevolence, there is peace. If it reigned throughout the universe, universal happiness would be the inevitable result. The happiness of heaven is perfect because benevolence is perfect there. The angels love God with all their heart, soul, mind and strength, and their neighbor as themselves. Perfect benevolence to God and man promotes happiness in earth and heaven.

Benevolence is good will. If we desire the welfare of others as much as we do our own, we are made as happy by good conferred on them as upon ourselves; and nothing but selfishness prevents our tasting the cup of everyone's happiness.

If we supremely desire the happiness and glory of God, our supreme joy will be the expectation that "the whole earth shall be full of his glory."

When we look upon mankind around the world and see all the wickedness, and through the pages of inspiration survey as with a telescope the deep caverns of the pit, when we listen to its wailings, behold the lurid flashes of its fires and contemplate the gnawings of the deathless worms, we see the legitimate results of selfishness. Selfishness is the discord of the soul, the jarring, dissonance and grating of hell's eternal anguish. Benevolence, on the other hand, is the melody of the soul; harmonizing all the mental powers so that they breathe the sweetness of heaven's charming symphonies. To be happy, then, you must be benevolent. Selfishness is neither reasonable nor profitable. Its very nature is at war with happiness and it renders you odious to God. It buries your good name, your ultimate self-esteem and your present and future happiness in one common grave. You are beyond the hope of resurrection unless you turn, renounce your selfishness and begin to obey the law of God.

PRINCIPLE 16

GOD SHOULD GOVERN US

Why should God govern the universe? In theory, you have perhaps never denied His right to govern. However, in practice you may have always denied it. Never having obeyed God is the strongest possible declaration of a person's denial of His right to govern. Your conduct may say, "Who is Jehovah, that I should obey Him? I know not Jehovah, neither will I obey His voice."

Have you considered why you should obey him? Your only conclusion would be that He has a right to govern. If you have never considered this question, it is not surprising that you have refused obedience. The foundation of God's right to govern the universe is made up of the three following considerations.

Reasons for God's Rule

1. *His moral character and natural attributes qualify Him to govern the universe.* His benevolence is infinite. Were He malevolent, He could have no right. It would be our duty to hate and disobey Him. But His benevolence renders Him worthy of our love and obedience. However, His benevolence alone cannot qualify Him to govern. However benevolent He may be, if His natural attributes were not sufficient He would not be qualified to be the Supreme Ruler of all worlds. But a glance at His natural attributes will show that He is no less worthy to govern in respect to these than in respect to His moral attributes.

He has infinite knowledge so that His benevolence will always be wisely exercised. He has infinite power. If He lacked either knowledge to direct or power to execute His desires, He would not be fit to govern. He is omnipresent, in every place at all times; so that nothing that benevolence desires, wisdom directs, or power achieves will be lacking in His administration. He is immortal and unchangeable. If He could cease to exist or were subject to change, there would be a fundamental defect in His nature as Supreme Ruler of the universe.

2. *He is the Creator.* When viewed separately or together, neither His moral nor natural attributes give sufficient ground for His assuming the reins of government. However good and great He may be, this is not sufficient reason for Him to take the office of governor, even if chosen by the other beings. But He also has the right to govern as Creator. He holds infinite tenure. Thus, He is infinitely qualified to govern, and by creation has the absolute and inalienable right to govern.

He has the right to govern, but it is also His duty to govern. He cannot yield this office nor throw aside this responsibility.

3. *His requirements are reasonable.* They are not arbitrary for He is bound to enforce them. The laws of God do not have their foundation in His arbitrary will, but in the nature and fitness of things as He created them. To love God and our neighbor is not our duty simply *because* He requires it; it was our duty prior to any expressed requirement. He requires it because it is right in itself. Therefore, He would not be at liberty to dispense with our obedience even if He pleased. He cannot good-naturedly humor His creatures and let them have their own way—let them run into sin and rebellion, and then let them go unpunished. He is solemnly pledged and bound by the rules of His own government.

God Has No Choice But to Punish Sinners

Therefore, if you continue in sin and come to the judgment, He does not have an arbitrary option to punish you or not. The laws of His empire are fixed, eternal principles which He can no more violate without sinning than any of His creatures. His

benevolence cannot allow the sinner to escape the damnation
of hell.

Perhaps you have made this excuse for your rebellion: "God
desires me to sin. Since He is almighty, He could prevent sin if
He pleased. Because He does not, He must prefer rebellion to
holiness." You have only to look into His law to see that He has
done all that He can to prevent the existence of sin. The rewards
of obeying His law are absolutely infinite; in it He has embodied
the highest possible motives to obedience. His law is moral and
not physical; a government of motive and not of force. It is vain
to talk of His omnipotence preventing sin; if infinite motives
will not prevent it, it cannot be prevented under a *moral government*.

Administering moral laws is not the object of physical
power. Therefore, to maintain that an all-powerful God could
prevent sin is nonsense. If swaying the intellect could be accomplished by the same power that sways the physical universe,
then indeed it would be reasonable to infer that God prefers the
existence of sin to holiness. But, since mind must be governed
by *moral* power, and the power of motive is all that can be
brought to bear upon it, it is unjust and illogical to infer that
God prefers sin.

Since the motives to obedience are infinite, He might chal-
lenge the universe and inquire, "What more could I have done
for my vineyard than I have done?" And will you, in the face of
all these considerations, continue your rebellion? When required to turn, will you profanely reply, "If God is Almighty,
why does He not turn me?" Oh, sinner, why provoke your
Maker? Your judgment does not linger and your damnation
does not slumber.

Jesus' Sacrifice Satisfies Justice

When the law was broken and mankind was exposed to its
fearful penalty, God offered justice to the universe and mercy
to sinners, which He displayed in the atonement. To make this
universal offer of pardon without regard to justice would violate
His law. A due regard for public interest forbade the Lawgiver

to forgive and set aside the penalty without finding a way to secure obedience to the law. Therefore, His compassion for mankind and His regard for the law was so great that He was willing to suffer in the person of His Son, who became a substitute for the penalty of the law. This was the most stupendous exhibition of self-denial that was ever made: the Father giving His only begotten and beloved Son; the Son veiling the glories of His uncreated Godhead and becoming obedient unto death, even the death of the cross, that we might never die.

Now, if you are unrepentant, you have never obeyed your Maker. Every step you have taken has added to your crimes. When God has fanned your heaving lungs, you have breathed out your poisonous breath in rebellion against Him. How should God feel toward you? You have walked over the principles of eternal righteousness with your unsanctified feet. You have lifted up your hands, filled with poisoned weapons, against the throne of the Almighty. You have spurned every principle of right, of love and of happiness. You are the enemy of God, the foe of man and a child of the devil in league with hell. Ought not God hate you with all His heart?

Yet, in the midst of your rebellion He has borne with you. All this you have done, and He has kept silent. Dare you think that He will never reprove?

The Conditions of the Gospel

Look for a moment at the conditions of the gospel: *repentance and faith*. To repent is to hate and renounce your sin. This requirement is not arbitrary. It would not be just or beneficial to you for God to pardon you before you repent. Can a king forgive His subjects while they remain in rebellion? Can God forgive you while you persevere in sin? He would have to give up His law and confess himself wrong and you right. But this would be falsehood, a proclamation that sin is right and holiness wrong. Not only this, but to forgive you and leave you in your sin would render your happiness impossible. A doctor might as well proclaim someone healthy who is dying with cancer.

Faith is not an arbitrary requirement of God. God has no means of getting you to heaven unless you believe His Word and walk in the path He points out. If you will not believe what He tells you of heaven and hell, of the way to avoid the one and gain the other, your salvation is impossible. You cannot find heaven at the end of the road that leads to hell. Only faith in what He tells you can influence you to take the path that leads to heaven.

Now if you are an unrepentant sinner, why should the sentence of His law not be executed upon you? You have never cared for God; why should He be under obligation to care for you? You have never obeyed Him; what good then do you deserve at His hand? You have broken His law, despised His grace and grieved His Spirit. "You have cast off fear and restrained prayer." Your selfish conduct has only tended to the ruin of the universe by dethroning God and establishing the dominion of Satan, damning yourself and all mankind. Let conscience pass sentence upon you. Do you not hear it crying out in the deep recesses of your soul, *guilty, guilty, and worthy of eternal death?*

PRINCIPLE 17

BE WILLING FOR GOD TO GOVERN YOU

You have seen the reasonableness of benevolence and the hatefulness of selfishness. If you are an unrepentant sinner, you must see the right and duty of God to govern you and your obligation to obey. You have seen the reasonableness and utility of virtue, and the guilt and evil of sin. Is it not right and honorable to turn and obey your Maker? Look at the consequences of your present course. Will you continue to cast firebrands and arrows, to throw all your influence, time, talents and your body and soul into the balance of selfishness? Do you want to continue to increase the wickedness and misery of earth, to gratify the devil and grieve the Son of God?

Sinner, if you go to hell, you ought to be willing to go alone. Taking friends with you will not mitigate your pain. It will increase it. Ought you not to throw all your influence into the other side of the balance now, to exert yourself to roll back the tide of death and save your fellowmen from hell? Do not stop to look at your emotions or turn your eye inward upon your present state of mind. Rather, cease your rebellion, throw down your weapons and enlist in the service of Jesus Christ! He has come to destroy the works of the devil, to demolish his empire and reestablish the government of God in the hearts of men. Are you willing that God should govern the world? If allowed to vote, would you elect Him as Supreme Governor of the world? Will you obey Him now?

Salvation Is a Question of Obedience

Do you say, "Oh! I am so great a sinner I fear there is no mercy for me"? The question is not whether He will pardon you, but whether you will obey Him. If it were not wise to pardon you and if His government required your damnation, it is still your duty to obey Him. The question for you to settle is whether you will obey Him or not. Leave the question of your salvation for Him to settle. He is infinitely wise and benevolent. You ought, therefore, to cheerfully submit your final destiny to Him, to make your duty the object of your attention and obedience your constant aim. The atonement is perfectly complete. Nothing stands in the way of your salvation but your own unrepentance and unbelief. You have the promise that on the condition of submission to His will, you shall have eternal life.

Do you see what you should do? Are you willing to do it? "Choose this day whom you will serve." To choose God and His service above your own interest is to change your heart. Have you done it? Or do you still ask, how shall I do it? You might more properly ask yourself, "How shall I go home from work?" To go home would require two things: first, to be willing; second, to put your body in motion. But here, no muscular power is needed; only a willing mind, your consent. Be willing to do your duty and the work is done.

You see why many complain that they cannot submit to God. They do not give their attention to the consideration necessary to lead them to submission. Many occupy their thoughts with their feelings. They look steadily at the darkness of their own minds and the hardness of their own hearts. They are anxiously waiting for the feelings which they suppose precede conversion. They will never submit like this. Their submission would counter all the laws of mind because their mental eye is turned away from the reasons for it.

Instead of thinking about the reasonableness of their Maker's claims, some give their whole attention to their own danger and try to submit out of fear, under the influence of self-love. They are not responding to the voice of conscience and justice. Actuated by such motives, the mind may struggle till the day of judgment without ever bringing the soul to true submission. True conversion comes when the soul responds to its duty and not to the danger of not fulfilling its duty. I have already said that both hope and fear bear an important part in leading the mind to make the required investigation; but neither one is the final reason for submission.

Therefore, he who does not understand the use and power of conscience and upon what to fix his mind to lead him to a right decision, will naturally complain that he does not know how to submit to God.

The Holy Spirit Leads the Sinner to Truth

Do you see the role of the Spirit of God in conversion? He operates through the medium of attention and conscience. He gets and keeps the attention of the mind, and through the influence of hope, fear and conscience, conducts the sinner along the path of truth. When He has given conscience the information to exert its power, then conscience gives forth its verdict and the will may respond—Amen.

This is the experience of every Christian. He knows that the Spirit of God exerted His influence to change his heart in this way. His errors and refuges of lies were swept away. The Spirit arrested his attention, enlightened his conscience and pressed truth upon his mind until he was induced to yield.

While pressing the sinner to submission, do you see how illogical it is to divert his mind to the Spirit's influence in conversion? While his attention is directed to that subject, his submission is impossible. He can only submit when his entire attention is directed to the reasons for submission. Every diversion of his attention is merely another obstacle in his way.

We never find the inspired writers directing attention to divine influence *when calling sinners to repent.* Joshua, when he assembled the people of Israel and reminded them of their duty, said, "Choose you this day whom ye will serve." He did not mention their dependence upon the Spirit of God. He held the single point upon which they were to choose before them until their choice was made. On the day of Pentecost, in the case of the Philippian jailer and in every other case where Christ, the prophets and the apostles called men to immediate repentance, we find them keeping close to their text and not going off to drag in the subject of divine influence to divert and confuse their hearers.

Do you see the importance of understanding the logic of conversion and why it is that so many sermons are lost upon the souls of men? The sinner's attention is not secured. If it is secured, it is often directed to irrelevant matters. The sermon contains many extraneous considerations that have nothing to do with the sinner's immediate duty. Often the subject is not clear in his mind; or if he understands it, he does not see its personal application to himself. If he sees this, he is not made to feel the immediate obligation to make a decision, and not infrequently—"Oh tell it not in Gath"—the impression is distinctly left that he is unable to do his duty. The preaching that leaves this last impression is infinitely worse than none at all.

You can see that *there are two classes of evidence of a change of heart. One class are the vivid emotions of love to God, repentance for sin and faith in Christ that often follow the change of choice.* These constitute happiness. They are highly prized and usually considered the most dependable, but are certainly not the most satisfactory. Highly wrought emotions are liable to deceive, for they are the least to be depended on as an evidence of conversion, since they cannot be examined without ceasing to exist. *The second class of evidence is an habitual disposition to obey the requirements of God, an abiding preference of God's glory over everything else which gives direction to our conduct.*

PRINCIPLE 18

NOW IS THE TIME TO DECIDE

Many people will set apart days of fasting and prayer, and spend the day examining their emotional state. They are sure to quench any right feeling they may have. They may examine their past thoughts, feelings, actions and motives, but whenever they make their present emotions the subject of attention, they cease to feel. Therefore, if you want to test your heart with regard to anything, bring that subject before your mind and consider it intensely. If there is any moral affinity between you and your focus of attention, then the fire of emotion will burn.

Some people suppose they have much more religion than others merely because they have more emotion. Multitudes uninfluenced by principle are carried hither and thither by every gust of emotion, no matter what may have produced the feelings. They tell of their raptures, love and joys but have so little regard for right principles that they are guilty of Christ-dishonoring conduct. Others may experience deep emotion only occasionally, and yet are influenced by a sacred regard to what is right. They have much more consistency of Christian character, but perhaps complain of an absence of religious joy.

If sinners continue to neglect the means of grace, their case is hopeless. Many seem to think that if they are to be saved they shall be saved, and if they are to be lost they shall be lost. They look upon religion as some mysterious thing; that they must wait for the whim of a sovereign God to implant religion in their minds. They pay attention to every other subject and occupy their thoughts with everything that is calculated to banish Christianity from their minds, and still hope to be converted. This is as irrational as a person desiring to obtain the perfection of Christian sobriety by reveling, drinking and stupifying his powers, still expecting that in some mysterious way he should by and by become a sober man.

The Fundamental Truths of Conversion Are Necessary

Do you see the importance of giving a convicted sinner right instructions? Great care should be taken not to divert his mind from fundamental truths. His attention should be pulled, if possible, from everything irrelevant, everything that regards merely the circumstantials of religion. His attention must be brought to bear intensely upon the main question of unconditional submission to God.

Very exciting means are often indispensable to awaken the sinner and secure sufficient attention to lead him to conversion. When there are many exciting topics continually before his mind to call and fix his thoughts on worldy things, it is necessary for us to ply him with the most moving thoughts in the most affectionate and earnest manner, or we shall fail to interest him and get the subject to his mind for consideration. If we can get to his mind, we can more easily touch the conscience.

Many people are averse to addressing the feelings of others on the subject of Christianity. They fear to excite emotions at all, so they generally excite no feeling at all. The reason is obviously this: they overlook some of the most striking peculiarities of the mind. They strive to arouse the conscience, but fail for lack of securing a person's attention. The attention will not ordinarily be secured without first addressing the hopes and fears of people.

Know the Difference Between *Convicted* and *Awakened*

We should carefully distinguish between a convicted and an awakened sinner. Once the sinner is awakened, there is then no need of creating further alarm. Appeals to hope and fear are then an embarrassment and hindrance to the progress of the work. When his attention is thoroughly secured, seize the chance to enlighten his mind with the claims of his Maker and a right understanding of his responsibilities. If his attention flags, appeals should be made to his feelings to rearouse and fix his thoughts; and watch to preserve attention and enlighten his mind as fast as possible. In this way you will most effectively aid the operations of the Holy Spirit, push matters to an issue and secure the conversion of the sinner to God.

Not distinguishing between awakening and conviction has been the cause of many failures in securing conversions. Often, merely awakened sinners have been treated as if they were convicted: their spiritual guides have not seized the opportunity to force conviction upon them. They have called on them to submit before they understood the reasons for submission or the nature of their duty. But instead of acting, they have imagined themselves willing to do so till their awakenings have subsided and the chill apathy of death has settled down upon them.

Preaching terror alone should not effect the conversion of sinners. It is useful to awaken, but if not accompanied with instructions that enlighten, it will seldom result in any good.

Those who preach only to the hopes of people seldom if ever effect their conversion. Some appeal to fear and others to hope, while they seldom reason with the sinner concerning righteousness or the judgment to come. They often excite feelings and many tears; but such appeals unaccompanied by discriminating instruction in regard to the sinner's duty and the claims of his Maker will seldom result in a sound conversion.

Do you see the necessity of special efforts to promote revivals of religion? Why there are protracted meetings to promote the conversion of sinners? Their novelty excites and fixes attention. Their continuation from day to day serves to enlighten the mind and has a tendency to result in conversion.

"People die as they live"

It can be seen that a death bed is a poor place for repentance. Many expect that if they neglect repentance until their last day that they shall then repent and give their hearts to God. But how vain the hope! In the anguish, exhaustion, pain, distraction and anxiety of a death bed, what opportunity or power is there for that intensity of attention that is needed to break the power of selfishness and change the entire current of the soul? To think is labor; to think intensely is exhausting labor, even to a man in health. But to understand the soul's destiny, to hold the agonized mind in distressing contact with the great truths of revelation until the heart is melted and broken is ordinarily too great an effort for a dying person. Be it known, with few exceptions, people die as they live. No trust can be placed upon the flickering and struggling mind while the body is breaking down to usher it into the presence of its Maker.

Now is your time to decide, in alertness and strength, while the command to make you a new heart and a new spirit is before you and the reasons for the performance of this duty lie clear. Decide while the gate of heaven stands open and mercy, with bleeding hands, beckons you to come. While the pearl of great price is offered for your repentance, seize the present moment and lay hold of eternal life.

PART 3

Traditions of the Elders

"Thus have ye made the commandment of God of none effect by your tradition"
(Matthew 15:6).

PRINCIPLE 19

GOD GOVERNS US THROUGH MOTIVES

God exercises a *moral government* over the mind. A *moral government* is not administered by direct physical agency. That would place the mind along with the material universe under the physical laws which operate in the world of matter. *Motives* are the great instruments for moving the mind.

God's moral government is made up of motivations designed to influence the minds of intelligent creatures to pursue that course of conduct which will, in the highest manner, promote the glory of God, as well as their own interests and the happiness of the universe. His government lays down a perfect rule for action. His precepts mark the exact course of duty. On the one hand, His rewards embrace all the blessedness of everlasting life; on the other, His disciplines damn offenders to all the pains of everlasting death. His moral government holds the clear lamp of truth before the sinner, revealing all the moving considerations that heaven, earth and hell can present to hold his mind in an exact course of obedience.

The law of God was clearly revealed to the Jews, but its influence over the mind was often paralyzed by a variety of oral traditions. These traditions were handed down from one generation to another, and were held as equal authority with the written law. Often they were the corrupt additions of the Jewish scholars, evasions of the spirit of the written law. We have an instance of this in the verses connected with the text.

The rabbis believed that it was unlawful to eat without first washing their hands. Christ's disciples paid no regard. But since the traditions were held in high regard by the multitude, the scribes and Pharisees made the disciples' unwashed hands an occasion for reproaching Christ. They demanded of Him, "Why do thy disciples transgress the tradition of the elders?" Christ rebuked them by answering, "Why do ye also transgress the commandment of God by your tradition? For God commanded, saying, honor thy father and mother, and he that curseth father or mother, let him die the death; but ye say, whosoever shall say to his father or mother, it is a gift, by whatsoever thou mightest be profited by me, and honoreth not his father and mother, he shall be free. Thus have ye made the commandment of God of none effect by your tradition." The commandment to honor father and mother included the duty of providing for them in case they were without means; however, the tradition of the elders evaded this requirement and taught that the child could give his property to God or dedicate it to religious purposes without making provision for his aged parents. By this evasion, they remained blameless; nullifying the requirement and setting aside the commandment of God.

Satan Tries to Confuse the Motives of the Gospel

Since the world began, Satan's policy has been to break the power of moral government. He has sought to introduce confusion, rebellion and damnation into the universe of God.

The influence of motive on the mind is in some respects similar to the law of gravitation in the material universe. Motivation is designed to hold the same place in the world of mind that gravitation holds in the world of matter. Universal desolation would be the consequence of breaking the power of gravitation. Destroy the power of motive, and universal anarchy and misrule will fill the universe. Therefore, everything which tends to hide the truth, to cloud the minds of people in ignorance, to give them erroneous notions of their duty before God and evasions and misrepresentations of the true nature and tendency of His commands are calculated to subvert their power and to defeat the very object for which they were made.

Thus, the corrupt glosses and traditional evasions of the Jews had blinded the Jewish nation. Their carnal interpretation of the law had so modified the views and doctrinal sentiments of the nation that they missed the nature of the Messiah's kingdom which they had so long expected. Even though the sacrifices of the ceremonial law were designed to point out the nature of the coming of Christ, these traditional delusions had been so great and their expectations of the Messiah so entirely erroneous that when He came, they did not know Him or His doctrine. They considered His claims as heresy. Hence, the nation rose up, rejected, persecuted and murdered Him. But after His resurrection and the pouring out of His Spirit on the day of Pentecost, the traditions of the Jewish doctors were discarded by the Christian Church.

The Unadulterated Truth Is Powerful

For a short time after Pentecost, the clear, unadulterated truth of God shone forth. It was powerful. Converts to Christianity were multiplied as drops of the morning dew. Judaism gave way before it. The systems of pagan idolatry shrank before its glories. Earth echoed back the hallelujahs of heaven. But in the midst of this bright day, even while some of the inspired penmen were yet alive, the corrupt philosophy of men began to break the power of truth. Men began to interpret the Scriptures by the corrupt standards of their philosophy. The truth became obscured, its influence over mind less and less manifest; until a day of darkness came which spread the pall of midnight over ages of history and peopled hell with millions of our race.

When Christians saw this darkness, instead of ascribing it to corruption, to human glosses and traditions that had broken the gospel's influence over mind, and inconsistencies with which man's traditions had encumbered the truth and palsied the arm of the church, they speculated. They sat quietly down and very learnedly endeavored to account for the fact that His glory had departed by ascribing the loss to the mysterious sovereignty of God.

These traditions multiplied in the Catholic Church until true conversion to God was hardly known among them. Many of these traditions were rejected by the Reformers, and light broke in again upon the world to break its slumbers. There is evidence that the Reformers' efforts brought many souls to Christ. But the Reformation was only partial. The gospel did not have its earlier effect. Since the glorious Son of righteousness was dimmed, something was evidently lacking, because through the gospel He had shined in full strength.

The systems of philosophy that still prevailed, standards by which people were interpreting the Word of God, introduced embarrassments, contradiction, mystery and absurdity into the gospel. The human mind was confounded, and a false philosophy has clogged the chariot wheels of His mercy to this day, and destroyed the power of the law.

PRINCIPLE 20

GOD'S LAW IS LOVING

We must know a few of the intents of the moral law and consider some of the traditions of men that have broken its power. The following are among the most obvious.

The Intentions of the Moral Law

The moral law is to exhibit the benevolence of God. A law expresses the will of the lawgiver. It is a declaration of his sentiments concerning his subjects, a portrait of his heart. We have only to look into the two great precepts that comprise the whole law and the prophets to learn that God is love. These command perfect love: supreme love to God and the same love to our fellows as we bear for ourselves. They are a universal rule of right for His kingdom. Universal obedience to these precepts would result in universal happiness.

God created us in His image. His happiness springs from His benevolent affections and so with us. Therefore, if everyone were benevolent as the law requires, universal good will, peace and joy would fill the earth.

The justice of God is also strongly exhibited in the law. The law calls man to reasonable and just love toward God, and perfect regard for the welfare of our fellowmen; nothing more nor less than is perfectly right.

Another intent of the moral law is *to convince people of sin.*

It does this by putting a perfect rule of action into people's hands, by holding strongly before their eyes a pure moral mirror that reflects the exact moral character of every thought, word and deed. It is the rule by which every action must be measured, the scale of the sanctuary in which every thought and affection must be weighed.

The moral law is also intended *to promote humility*. By comparing his life and affections with this holy law, the sinner finds that everything is wrong. On being weighed in this balance he finds himself lacking. His self-complacency is destroyed and his pride is humbled.

The moral law is designed *to destroy self-righteousness and teach men their need of an atonement and a Savior.*

Another intention of God's law is *to promote holiness and happiness among people.* We must be shown the impossibility of being happy without first being holy; that without perfect holiness no one shall see the Lord. The moral law impresses upon our hearts and consciences our obligation to perfect benevolence, and convicts us of sin in every instance in which we come short of it.

In short, God's law is obviously designed to declare the perfection of God and the total depravity of man. For since it is a faithful portrait of the perfection of God's moral character on the one hand, so it is a faithful witness of the entire depravity of man on the other.

Traditions Have Altered the Law

Yet, all these intents of the moral law have been defeated by the traditions of men. Pharisees, both of the ancient and modern variety, have defeated these designs by altering the precept. Some of them have made obedience a mere *outward* conformity to the law of God, regardless of the state of the heart, while the law principally regards the heart rather than the outward act. The law judges the heart, the intention with which an action is performed. It gives no credit for outward action unless it proceeds from a right purpose. The act must be prompted by love, at the bidding of holy principle, to be recognized as virtue by the law of God.

Does a man pray or preach or give alms to the poor? Does he read his Bible or go to church? Unless these are prompted by the love of God in his heart, they are neither obedience nor virtue. Still the law thunders forth its claims, *thou shalt love the Lord thy God with all thy heart, with all thy soul, with all thy mind, and with all thy strength, and thy neighbor as thyself.* No outward conduct, however sanctimonious or precise, is to be regarded as obedience to the law of God unless it flows from love. Obviously, merely making outward morality conform to this law defeats one of its principal designs. Instead of convicting of sin, it fosters pride. Instead of exhibiting the true character of God, it holds Him forth merely as the promoter of cold, dry morality. Instead of making people humble and showing them their need of a Savior, it leads to self-complacency, stumbling at the doctrine of atonement and misunderstanding and rejecting the gospel.

This false view of the moral law (that it regards the outward action primary) was so extensively embraced by the Pharisees that it led the Jewish nation to reject and crucify the Savior. They rejected the righteousness of God and tried to establish their own righteousness by an outward conformity to the law. Assuming obedience to the law, how could they understand the need of an atonement, the righteousness of Christ and justification by faith alone? So it is with the Pharisees of today: overlooking the inwardness of God's law and supposing their cold, dry, outward morality to be approved in the sight of God, they wrap the filthy garments of their own righteousness about themselves, walk in the light of their own fire and warm themselves with sparks of their own kindling—they must lie down in sorrow.

PRINCIPLE 21

GOD'S LAW IS POSITIVE

Some people make the moral law ineffective by regarding it only negatively. They believe that God designed it to prohibit the outbreaking of positive selfishness. They do not regard His law as requiring positive benevolence and virtue. These people go no further than speaking dramatically against gross sin. Since they regard the law simply as prohibitory, they resist the tide of corruption as it flows from the deep fountain of their hearts. Yet they say nothing of the positive character of the law as requiring every creature of God to *devote all his powers to His service*, give himself up to doing good and promoting the interests of Christ's kingdom.

By necessity, the religion of these people is merely negative. Since they believe they do nothing very evil, since they abstain from those sins that would disgrace them in the eyes of men, they imagine themselves to be Christians. They know they do nothing benevolent. They do not deny themselves, take up their cross daily to follow Christ, hold all their possessions as mere stewards or account their time and talents as belonging to Christ to be used only for His glory. Yet they think they are Christians. They know that they effect little or no good in the world, but they content themselves with avoiding gross evil. They call themselves Christians on the basis of a fundamental mistake with regard to the nature of the law of God. A proper view of the law would annihilate these false hopes, sweep away their refuge of lies and bring them to a better understanding of God and of themselves.

Obviously, much of what is called "Christianity" in the present age is this negative piety. Ask a person who professes faith in Christ if he is doing any real positive good, and if he is of this camp and truly honest he will tell you no, not that he knows of—but he will also declare that he is doing nothing very bad. Thus, the high claims of the law are set aside, its design is perverted and the hypocrite rests quietly in his sins.

The Moral Law Can Only Be Fulfilled in the Gospel

Another group, the *Antinomians*, void the law. *Antinomian* is a compound word from Greek roots meaning "without law." The sect originated in the days of the Apostles. Its followers suppose that the gospel was designed to release Christians from their obligation to obey the moral law. Their doctrine grew out of a perversion of the doctrine of justification by faith.

The Jewish scholars had taught that men would be saved only by perfect outward conformity to the moral and ceremonial laws. In opposition to this, Paul taught that by the works of the law no flesh can be justified; first, because all men had broken the law already, and second, because no obedience however perfect could make restitution for past disobedience.* Therefore, all people are already condemned by the law because of their sins. *Justification* in the New Testament is synonymous with *pardon and acceptance. The atonement of Christ is, therefore, the only ground of pardon. Those who are saved are justified solely by faith in Christ irrespective of any legal righteousness of their own.*

The biblical view of justification was perverted by the Antinomians. They maintained that if people were justified by

---

*We must continually bear this teaching of Paul in mind, and not become confused when Finney insists that we are able to obey the law of God. Finney agrees with Paul. Any subsequent obedience to the law of God will not justify us; however, even with our limited powers we are able to love God with all our heart, mind, soul, and strength, and our neighbor as ourselves. See *Principles of Sanctification* for a further explanation of why Christians can and must obey the law of God.

faith alone, then good works are unnecessary. They believed that faith in Christ is substituted for obedience to the law of God. They overlooked the fact that without personal holiness no one shall see the Lord.

Holiness of Heart Is Part of the Gospel

Varieties of the Antinomian sect have existed throughout history and in almost every part of the Church. They have not always been known by this name, but thousands have and still do manifest their beliefs and practices. They may generally be recognized; when holiness of heart and life are demanded, they complain that this is legal preaching, that the gospel has been exchanged for the law. They think that the gospel is designed to repeal the moral law; not only to set aside the penalties for believers in Christ, but also to discharge them from any obligation to obey the law. They array Christ and His gospel against the moral government of God, render it impossible for either law or gospel to sanctify them and "utterly perish in their own corruption."

Obviously, a person professing faith in Christ must live a holy life, *as holy as if* he expected to be saved by his works. If he indulges in sin, abandoning all regard for the law, he is turning the grace of God into licentiousness and making Christ the minister of sin. He is perverting and abusing the gospel. He becomes, in heart, an Antinomian. The gospel becomes license to sin and Christ the apologist for sin, saving those who make His gospel the ground for committing those sins which they would not dare commit if they depended upon their own obedience for justification.

PRINCIPLE 22

UNIVERSALISM IS DANGEROUS

Some destroy the power of the law by denying its penalty. The penalty is the lawgiver's motive to induce obedience; the greater the penalty, the more influential the motive to obey. Delete the penalty entirely, and you destroy all motivation for obedience, except what is contained in the nature of the precept. The precept without a penalty is no law at all, only advice which may be received or rejected at pleasure.

Two kinds of Universalists nullify the power of moral government by dismissing the penalty of the law. There are *no-hellites*, and *limitarians* or *restorationists*. The *no-hellites* maintain that people neither deserve nor receive any other punishment for sin than what they receive in this life. The *limitarians* declare that there will be a limited punishment in a future world; when sinners have been punished according to their sins, they will be translated from hell into heaven. Both sects believe that all mankind will ultimately be saved.

The *no-hellites* completely set aside the *penalty* of the law of God, and regard the sufferings of this life as the *natural* and only consequences of sin to man. The *limitarians* fritter away the penalty and reduce it to an indefinable something, the amount or duration of which they do not pretend to know. The penalty is finite, infinitely less than eternal. It is infinitely less solemn, awful, impressive, commanding and influential than an eternal penalty.

The Penalty Motivates Obedience

I have said that the rewards and punishments of moral law are designed to hold the same place in the moral or spiritual world that the law of gravitation does in the material world. The mode of their operation is not the same. Gravitation is a law of matter and can only be administered by force. Moral law operates on the mind and is designed to secure voluntary obedience. As the law of gravitation holds the sun, moon, and planetary system in their courses, so the motives of moral government are designed to preserve moral agents voluntarily under the government of God.

While the reality of the penalty was kept before the mind of Adam, he obeyed; but as soon as his confidence in that penalty was lost, he fell. Annihilate the law of gravitation, and sun, moon and planets rushing from their orbits would wreak havoc throughout the universe. So he, as soon as the force of moral government had been broken, rushed from the orbit of his obedience and filled the world with groans and desolation.

The Universalists desire to relieve the world of its anxieties, by infinitely mitigating the penalty of the law of God. If they could succeed in convincing everyone of their beliefs, they would completely annihilate the power of moral government. If all believed that God never threatened men with *eternal* death, that the sufferings of this world are all that sin deserves and that God never intended to punish in a future world, would this sentiment promote obedience to the law of God? If we take away the penalties for disobeying human laws will we secure obedience to them?

Law Without Penalty Is Lawlessness

Suppose a politician went through his country maintaining that legal penalties were wholly unnecessary, that it was better not to threaten people with evil for disobedience. Suppose he advocated that the government need only exhibit its love of virtue, its mildness and humanity. Suppose he said that the penalty for murder was entirely unnecessary; that the accusations of conscience that remembering a crime would bring upon its perpetrator were as much as the crime deserved. Would he not be regarded as a madman fit for bedlam? Would not everyone regard his doctrine as dangerous or ridiculous? Would he do the world a favor by persuading it to strike out the penalties of all their laws? Would he not be regarded as an enemy of the human race, aiming to open the flood gates of iniquity and inundate the world with crime?

Even though the death penalty is not in all cases sufficient to prevent murder, it is logically sound. Is it common sense that to mitigate its pains or to substitute a lesser motive would be sufficient to prevent the crime? But even the penalty of eternal death does not restrain all from sin. This infinite penalty has not sufficient weight to counteract the selfishness of the human heart. By what mad logic do some arrive at the sage conclusion that doing away with the penalty would have a tendency to promote obedience to God?

It is in vain to say that the excellence of the law without the penalty is a sufficient motive to secure obedience. This is not only illogical but also contrary to experience. There is a powerful motive in the precept itself: the happiness of virtue. But the nature of the mind demands not only rewards for obedience but penalties for evil. This is especially obvious in a universe where virtue is to be tested by temptation.

If Universalists could succeed in establishing the doctrine of the serpent, that the wicked shall not die, then they would make the commandment of God ineffective and introduce universal rebellion into the empire of God. If an *infinite* penalty does not sufficiently restrain the selfishness of the human heart, what delirious babble is it to say that a *finite* one would?

Fear Appeals to Self-love

Some say that the penalty of eternal death only appeals to fear, that men cannot be frightened into obeying God. The truth is, both fear and hope are innate in the human mind, both are implanted there as principles upon which moral government can act. *Self-love*, or the love of happiness and dread of misery, differs entirely in its nature from selfishness. Both law and the gospel continually make their appeals to hope and fear.*

We have before us a striking illustration of the death blow given by Universalist sentiments to the law of God. Their preaching of a universal salvation never makes people more holy, never convinces of sin and promotes revivals of religion, and never engages men in prayer and mission effort. Who ever knew the law of God, robbed of its penalty, to reform a drunkard, rebuke and reclaim an adulterer or bring the high-handed sinner to his knees and humble him as a little child.

There is no tendency in Universalism to reform mankind. This is logically plain and abundantly established by facts. They may exhibit their traditions till the day of judgment, but instead of promoting holiness, they will only open the flood gates of iniquity.

---

*For a further exposition of hope and fear in relation to the gospel, see "Legal Experience" and "Religion of the Law and the Gospel" in Finney's *Principles of Victory*: sermons from Romans; and "License, Bondage and Liberty" in *Principles of Liberty*: more sermons from Romans.

PRINCIPLE 23

FALSE INTERPRETATIONS ARE DANGEROUS

The gospel has been weakened by the traditions of men. Too many teachers have overlooked its two-fold design. *First*, the gospel is designed to establish the moral law. The gospel requires the same holiness of heart and life as the moral law. It aims at restoring people to perfect obedience. It does not abrogate or repeal the law, but enforces obedience by exhibiting the original rewards and penalties of the law while adding the unique ones of the gospel.*

Second, the gospel is designed to offer pardon on terms that are consistent with the honor of the moral Governor, and to promote the stability of His government. Failure to promote either of these two intentions is to render the gospel ineffective.

Some have taught that the gospel is merely a system of mercy, that it offers pardon for sin irrespective of any intention to make people holy in this life. They have made the gospel ineffective by making it a *remedy* without convincing the sinner that he needs healing. They have urged the sinner to accept a pardon without convincing him of his guilt. Thus perverted, the gospel has no power to save man. By overlooking gospel morality, its mercy and its pardon cannot save souls. Justifi-

---

*See Finney's *Principles of Holiness* for his excellent series of sermons on holiness of heart and life.

cation without sanctification or forgiveness without holiness is absurd, and salvation upon such conditions is impossible.

Some of these teachers lay great stress upon the atonement, and even admit the divinity of Jesus Christ, but they exalt a dead faith above obedience to the law of God. These professing Christians are generally known by their great zeal for what they call "sound doctrine." But they are reluctant to hear the self-denying duties of the gospel forcibly taught. The doctrines of God's sovereignty, the perseverance of the saints and doctrines like these are the only truth which they relish; and only a distorted view of these can feed them. They lay much more stress on "doctrine" than on the practice of doctrine, which is the sole object of sound doctrine to produce. They rest on the shadow and reject the substance. They are hearers, but not doers of the word, deceiving their own selves. They shall utterly perish in their own corruption.

Powerless Good Works

Another tradition professes to recognize the morality of the gospel, but denies the power of faith and the atonement of the Son of God. The power of the gospel is sadly marred; they deny its motivations and annihilate its power. The gospel's most moving motive is presented in the atonement. Blot out this, and it has no power to save.

Both of these traditions are equidistant from the truth. The one denies the morality, and the other rejects the leading motives; thus the power of the blessed gospel is destroyed. Adherents of both systems are yet in their sins. The one admits the gospel's morality but rejects the atonement for a system of self-righteousness. The other admits the atonement but overlooks the need of personal holiness and turns the grace of God into licentiousness.

The Indwelling Element of Sin

Others have broken the power of the gospel by introducing traditions which make it less attractive. One tradition preaches the doctrine of "physical depravity" or "physical sinfulness": in other words, depravity or sinfulness is physical; it enters into the very substance of the human soul. This doctrine says that physical depravity causes a natural desire for sin, much as the natural desire for food that we have in the body.

Founded upon this doctrine is the tradition of "inability" on the part of of the sinner to accept the gospel. Some people maintain that the sinner is no more able to embrace the gospel than he is to create a world. They call on sinners to repent and believe, but are careful to tell them that they cannot. Thus, as some have humorously said, they preach:

You can, and you can't,
You shall, and you shan't,
You will, and you won't,
You'll be damned, if you don't.

A related dogma is "physical regeneration." This is the ultimate end of this system of belief, for if our nature itself is depraved or sinful, if depravity is something physically created in the person, then regeneration must remedy the physical defect. The people who preach this say that conversion destroys the constitutional craving for sin and alters the powers of moral agency so that obedience and holiness will be possible.

No greater obstacles could be presented to the reception of the gospel than these three dogmas: physical depravity, inability, and physical regeneration. They all lead logically to the exercise of ι spirit of self-justification. A person has no right to blame himself for his sinfulness if it is physical. He ought to justify himself, and to repent of such depravity is impossible. A man might as well be called upon to repent of the color of his skin, of the color of his eyes, or for any of the bodily senses which he possesses. If his depravity is constitutional, is it just or possible for him to repent of his actual transgressions? If they are the natural results of a depraved and defective body, he is no more to blame for them than for the effects of any bodily disease with which he may have been born.

Can we trust a gospel which demands a sinner to repent of constitutional depravity or suffer eternal death? And, to complete the absurdity and insult, it informs him at the same time that he has no power to repent and believe the gospel. To tantalize him with salvation upon impossible conditions both insults his understanding and mocks his hopes. Is this the gospel of the blessed God? Impossible! It is a libel upon the Almighty!

The Waiting System

A tragic, but inevitable, tendency of these traditions is to lead those who embrace them to adopt the *waiting system*. If the sinner is really unable to obey God, of what use are his efforts? He must quietly wait for God to change his heart. This is the inevitable deduction from these false premises. He can deduct that God alone is to blame for his continued unrepentance and disbelief.

Universalism is, unfortunately, the inferred result from these dogmas. If someone assumes that people are physically unable to obey the gospel and must wait for physical regeneration, he must either conclude that God is an infinite tyrant or that all will be saved.

These traditions have an obvious tendency to conduct a thinking mind into infidelity. "What!" exclaims a man of thought. "Am I to believe that a book containing such absurdities as these is from God; that God has made men sinners, incapable of serving Him, and suspends their salvation upon impossible conditions, damning them if He does not help them comply with these impossible conditions? Monstrous! Blasphemous! Who can believe this!" Having neither desire nor perhaps time to examine the Bible for himself, he naturally concludes that if these are the doctrines of the Bible, its religion is but a sham.

These dogmas have produced dreadful rebellion against Almighty God. Sinners, supposing these to be the true teachings of Scripture, have been led to curse God to His face. But their opposition to God is natural, considering their assumptions.

Conversion Without Choice

The last tradition which I shall mention is what is generally called "irresistible grace." This doctrine maintains that sinners are irresistibly converted; that if they are of the elect, they will be converted in spite of themselves. "Irresistible grace" cannot be resisted.

Nothing quiets a sinner more than the idea of irresistible grace in regeneration. Do what he will and resist as he will, if he is to be converted he will be saved. I cannot conceive of anything more directly intended to break the power of the gospel and settle sinners down until they sink to the depths of hell.

In many instances these traditions of physical sinfulness, inability and physical regeneration have led people to justify themselves and condemn God. Hence, when they have been called to repent and believe the gospel, they have replied that they were willing but waiting for God to do it. A compromise ensued.

Instead of calling sinners to immediate repentance, they have been told to use the means of grace, to call upon God for the influence of His Spirit and wait for sovereign grace to change their hearts. Their consciences have been relieved and the obligation mitigated. They pray themselves to sleep and sink to the depths of hell.

The Gospel Demands Immediate Response

The requirement of the gospel is *repent now* and believe, that your soul may live. The gospel does not give the sinner a moment's delay. The weight of God's authority presses him to instantly lay down his weapons and submit to God. He feels hedged in as with a wall of fire; he pants, struggles and is driven to extremity. He prays, goes to church, reads his Bible and attends to the means of grace, but his conscience finds no relief; for the gospel still thunders *repent and believe*. The requirement follows him and increases his distress.

But here comes the soothing opiate of the doctrine of inability. He meets someone who tells him that God is a sovereign, that he cannot repent himself, that if he prays and waits for God's time, he has every reason to hope that God will change his heart. "Ah," says the sinner, "Is it so? I feel relieved. I felt as if ten thousand voices were crying *repent, repent!* in my ears.

The more I prayed, the more guilty I felt. I *supposed* that God required nothing less than absolute submission. But I thank you for your comforting word. If this is all, to wait God's time, I can do it without distraction."

Another requirement has been substituted for God's and the power of the gospel has been broken. The sinner breathes easier, relieved from the pressure of obligation, drinks the lethal draught of the soul-killing poison and goes down to hell.

The more industriously the sinner uses the means of grace in his new state of peace, the less real conviction of sin he will have. The more he repeats his impenitent prayers, the more acceptable he must suppose himself to be to God. Thus, his fears gradually subside; his self-righteousness increases, his delusions deepen, his conscience is stifled and he will cry *peace and safety* when sudden destruction comes upon him that he cannot escape.

PRINCIPLE 24

RIGHT VIEWS ARE ESSENTIAL FOR REVIVAL

Can you see why some deny the doctrine of total depravity? There are two principal reasons. Some confine their attention to the prohibitory applications of God's law, as contained in the Ten Commandments. This overlooks the positive perfection that the law commands in thought, word and deed. They substitute another rule of conduct by comparing themselves with a false standard. Instead of carefully weighing their thoughts and affections in the delicate scales of the sanctuary under the clear blaze of the law of God, they use their own corrupt scale and sink down to death.

Others deny the doctrine of total depravity because they cannot understand how the *created powers* of the mind should be sinful *in themselves*; how a God of justice could make people with a totally depraved *nature*. Nor can I. If this is what is meant by depravity, I not only deny total depravity, but all depravity.

Do you understand why some see no need of an atonement for sin? They have entirely misunderstood the nature of God's law. This was the reason why the scribes and Pharisees had no notion of the need for an atonement. Their system was mere self-righteousness. Therefore, they called the Deity of Jesus Christ and the doctrine of His atonement blasphemous.

The doctrine of grace should lead to morality. Some have

regarded the vicarious sufferings of Jesus Christ and His atonement for sin as dangerous doctrines designed to encourage people in iniquity by preserving the hope of heaven for them, even though they may continue in rebellion against God to the last hour of their lives. Thus, they view the doctrine of grace as intended to overthrow the very foundations of morality and dangerous to the well-being of society. But the fact is, as experience shows, those who embrace the doctrine of grace exhibit the purest morality.

The reason for this is that even though they understand the gospel to demand repentance and faith, they still regard God's law as the rule of their lives. They keep their eye upon the law as a mirror to see their exact moral image. This leads them to watchfulness, to prayer and walking with God. While the purity of its precepts annihilates every hope of salvation by their own works, they feel that until they are perfectly conformed to the full length and breadth of the law's requirements, they cannot be perfectly happy.

Those who depend upon their own works and the mercy of God for salvation exhibit a spurious and lax morality. Their vague notions about God's law, which lies at the foundation of their rejecting the doctrine of atonement, and their sense of duty, will make their morality defective.

The Gospel Is to Bring Sinners Back to Obedience to the Law

Do you see why some who call themselves Christians, when their sins are pointed out and they are required to obey the law of God, cry out, "This is not the gospel. This is law. Tell us of the mercy of God. We want to hear about Christ, not about the law"? Such people are Antinomians. They regard the gospel simply as a system of pardon and overlook its great design to make them holy and bring them back to perfect obedience to the law.

From this we may understand why the gospel has had so little influence over the minds of men for so many hundred years. For many centuries, little of the real gospel has been preached. So much has been intermingled with it that its power has been broken. All the errors and false notions that have grown out of the doctrine of physical depravity have served to shield the sinner from the arrows of the Almighty. Physical depravity, physical regeneration, the sinner's inability and all their kindred errors have formed hiding places under which millions upon millions have entrenched themselves. They are groaning in hell because these traditions have made void the commandment of God.

The gospel is intended to bring people to immediate repentance, nothing *short of this*. But some who have believed that sinners are unable to do this have set them to do something which God never required as a condition of salvation. They have put off repentance, sinned away their day of grace and lost their souls.

The Gospel's Power Is in Its Purity

The gospel was early corrupted. These corruptions have continued to mingle with the pure gospel; and precisely in proportion to the error mingled with the truth, the gospel has been more or less successful. Its power depends on its purity.

Multitudes have preached the substance of the gospel, but they have added something of their own. They have boldly called on people to repent, but before they left the pulpit, they were sure to admonish them that they had no power to obey God. Suppose the Apostles had done this on the day of Pentecost. When the alarmed Jews cried out, "Sirs, what shall we do to be saved," instead of saying, "Repent every one of you," they would have said, "You can't repent, you are dependent upon the Spirit of God. You must pray, use the means of grace and wait God's time." If the multitude had believed them, not one of them would have been converted on the spot.

The earth's redemption can never come until all the dogmas that afford hiding places for the enemies of God are rejected as no part of the gospel of Christ. When ministers of all denominations shall see eye to eye, shall disencumber the gospel of all these traditions, take the pure commandment of God and bring it with an uncompromising spirit to bear with mountain weight upon the rebellious hearts of dying men; when they call on them to instantly repent and treat them as if he expected them to; when they live, labor, pray and preach the gospel in all they say and do; then, and not till then, will the full power of God's moral government be felt on earth.

These traditions are the sources of most of the fatal errors of the present day. Universalists have based their notions on the doctrines of inability and physical depravity. They have reasoned, "If men were created with a depraved nature, physically and naturally inclined to all evil, unable to obey God, then surely a God of justice cannot condemn them." From their premises, this is only logical. For God to make people physically incapable of obedience, and then damn them for disobedience would be infinite tyranny and injustice. In light of physical depravity, God's love and justice logically result in Universalism. There is no place for mercy, for there is no just condemnation.

The Sinner Must See His Selfishness

But take away the foundation, and the superstructure falls. Annihilate the dogma of physical depravity and inability, show the sinner that his wicked heart is the result of his *voluntary selfishness* and his rejection of God; show him that he is blamed for his *conduct* and not his *nature*, for his *will not* and not his *cannot*, and you will destroy the very foundation upon which his Universalism is built. You will convince him of his sin, and shut him up to the faith of Christ.

Do you see the foundations of modern infidelity in the doctrine of physical depravity? Thinking people, hearing those doctrines so often from the pulpit, become disgusted when, in the same breath, they hear people called upon to repent and told that they cannot repent. When they hear the doctrine of the new birth covered with mystery, they look upon it as absurd and conclude that it is all a sham.

It is easy to see why revivals cannot prevail more than they do. These crippling errors are so firmly entrenched that the influence of a great portion of the church is paralyzed. Many good people are doubting whether they should reject them or not. Others come out boldly for these dogmas, but while they are held before the mind, it cannot be expected that revival should prevail. It is true that some men who have held these views have had powerful revivals, but their preaching took effect when they *did not* exhibit these doctrines. Fortunately, they were inconsistent enough to lay aside these peculiarities and preached the powerful gospel upon the hearts and consciences of men; and they had revival.

Let me tell you a parable. A lady, who had been under conviction a long time, had often called on her minister to know what she should do to be saved. He had always reminded her of her helplessness and dependence upon God, and exhorted her to pray, to use the means of grace and wait patiently for God to change her heart. On Sunday he would frequently call upon sinners to repent, always careful to caution them against depending upon their own strength. But one day he sat down after pressing sinners to immediate repentance, forgetting the usual addition that they could not. Before the last hymn had concluded, the gospel had done its work in the woman's heart. After the service, she wept as she walked out to speak with him. She met him and exclaimed, "My dear Pastor, why did you not tell me of this before?" "Tell you of this before?" questioned the astonished pastor. "I have declared it to you every Sunday." "Yes," she replied, "but you have always told us, before you sat down, that we could not repent." "I hope," said the pastor, "you have not gone on in your own strength." "No," she replied, "not in my own, but in the strength of God I have repented, and would have done it before had you not told me that I could not."

This is the result of the doctrine of "cannotism." If people believe it, they certainly will not repent. How can revival prevail? These dogmas have become fundamental doctrines, and those who do not hold to them are supposed to be heretics. Christ could easily turn upon the real heretics with the rebuke, "Wherefore do ye make void the commandment of God by your traditions."

PART 4

Total Depravity

"But I know you, that ye have not the love of God in you" (John 5:42).
"The carnal mind is enmity against God, for it is not subject to the law of God, neither can be" (Romans 8:7).

PRINCIPLE 25

CAREFULLY DEFINE YOUR TERMS

I need to establish the biblical view of the doctrine of total depravity. In the following principles, I will show what the doctrine of total depravity is not, then what it is and finally I will prove it.

Total depravity is not a lack of faculties to obey God. We have all the powers of moral agency that we need to render perfect obedience to God. If our natures lacked any moral faculties, our responsibility would cease. If we do not possess the appropriate moral powers, we cannot be justly blamed for disobedience.

Total depravity does not consist in a mutilated state of our moral powers. If they were mutilated, our obligation to obedience would be diminished in proportion to the imperfections of moral agency.*

Total depravity is not physical pollution transmitted from Adam, through our ancestors, to us. Some speculate that there is an evil physical element incorporated with the substance of our being. But, it is utter nonsense that moral depravity should be physical. It would not be *moral*, but *physical* depravity. It could not be a *sinful* depravity. It would be a *disease*, and not a *crime*.

---

*Finney discusses in-depth how our fallen nature with its diminished powers relates to perfect obedience to the law of God, the law of love, in *Principles of Sanctification*.

Total depravity is not a principle of sin that is incorporated *into* our being. The word *principle* is used in two senses. It sometimes means an attribute which has an inherent tendency to produce results agreeable to its nature. In this sense, depravity is not a principle, not an attribute of any substance. It is not part of either body or mind, but part of the character.

Principle also means purpose, preference, disposition, or voluntary inclination. *In this sense,* depravity is a principle; but in no other sense.

Total depravity does not mean that any person is sinful before he has chosen to do wrong.

Total depravity is not the disposition to sin belonging to the substance of body or mind. This would be the same as the serpent's instinct to bite or the wolf's to devour sheep. There is not a constitutional appetite or craving for sin implanted in the substance of the body or mind.

Total depravity does not mean that people are as bad as they can be. If they were placed under less restraint or greater temptation, they would doubtless be worse than they are.

Man Is Completely Depraved

People misunderstand the word *total* to signify the highest possible degree of depravity. But certainly this is not the meaning of the word *total*. The sum total of 3 and 2 and 5 is 10. This is not the highest possible number, but it is the total of 3 and 2 and 5. *Total,* when qualifying depravity, does not mean the highest possible degree, but simply the completeness of the depravity. *The whole character is depraved*: there is no mixture of good in man. Not that he does and says as wickedly as he could do and say, but that whatsoever he does and says is sinful: "That every thought and imagination of his heart is only evil continually."*

Jesus said of some, "But I know you, that ye have not the love of God in you," asserting that sinners do not have the love

---

*See the principle of the unity of moral action in *Finney's Systematic Theology* (Minneapolis: Bethany House Publishers, 1976).

of God in them. It would be easy to show that this is recognized everywhere in the Bible. But since I must deal with people whom I affirm to be totally depraved, I do not expect that a *thus saith the Lord* will settle the question. There is an exhaustless variety of other proofs within my reach, and I will lay a few of them before you for consideration.

Facts are stubborn things. People may evade the Bible, but they find it difficult to resist plain matters of fact, especially when the facts come from their own experience. I want to point out facts in your own history and the history of those around you that will place this doctrine upon a solid foundation.

We Delight in Pleasing Whom We Love

The laws of mind are still imperfectly understood. Yet, certain laws are understood even by children. For instance, by experience we know that we delight in pleasing the object of our affection: to love an individual is to desire his happiness. It is not essential that we aim at satisfying ourselves; for to make him happy makes us happy.

When we act virtuously, pleasing ourselves is not a part of our ultimate purpose. But although pleasing ourselves does not enter into our design, it is the natural result of pleasing another whom we love. Satisfying our desire to promote his happiness, satisfying the one we love, is happiness.

We find this principle in life. When is the affectionate husband or wife more happy than when they are engaged in something that makes the other happy? Lovers and other dear friends never tire in their efforts to please their companions. They eagerly anticipate each other's desires. It is a contradiction for you to say that you love someone and have no delight in pleasing him. To say that you love a person is the same as saying that you desire his happiness.

This law of mind holds true in Christianity. I appeal to every Christian reading this, whether it is not your meat and drink to do the will of your Heavenly Father. When are you as happy as when engaged in those things that you know will promote the honor and glory of God? I do not mean that your *design* is to satisfy yourself when you obey and serve God. But I ask, do you not find it to be a matter of fact that you are happier pleasing God than doing anything else? You search His Word to know what will please Him. When you know His will, you do it for His sake; but you know that the performance of duty promotes your own happiness. To please God, pleases you.

To Love God Is to Please Him

Let me appeal to the experience of every unrepentant sinner. You understand that you love to please your friends. How you delight to satisfy your children, to please those whom you love! But I ask your conscience, *do you take delight in pleasing God?* Do you seek to know what will please Him? When you have learned His will, do you perform it?

Everything you say or do is viewed in relation to the object of supreme affection. If you love money supremely, everything is hated or loved according to your own pecuniary interest. If you can make money by it, you have pleasure in it. If it would delete your wealth, you are displeased with it. Your conduct is modified and all your pursuits are regulated by this controlling and absorbing affection for your idol.

I ask you again, is it true that everything pleases or displeases you, according to its relation to the will of God? If not, why do you pretend to love God? You would not believe that your children or wife loved you unless you saw that they delighted to please you. Why should you deceive yourself by supposing that you love God when you know it is not your happiness to please Him?

PRINCIPLE 26

KNOW WHAT TRUE LOVE IS

Our minds are such that we delight in the company and conversation of those we greatly love. To be alone with them, to enjoy their confidence and to pour out our hearts to them are some of the sweetest joys. This law of mind is true also in religion.

Saints have always delighted to commune with God. They are never happier than when alone in secret and holy communion with the blessed God. Now, sinner, is this your experience? Do you love to be alone with God? Do you delight to pray? I do not ask you whether you pray, for this you may do from a variety of motives, but is it because you love to pray? Because you love to commune with God? If you are an unrepentant sinner, you know that you do not love the company of God.

We Seek the Approval of the People We Love

We naturally prize the approval of one we love. We deem it indispensable to our own happiness. We are so created that it gives us great pain to know that our conduct is disapproved of by our dearest friends: both our worldly friends and God. Nothing will wring a Christian's heart with more intolerable anguish than the conviction that his conduct merits the disapproval of God. (In most cases this is not because of any fear of punishment.) He will not fear punishment, but he has offended

God! He is ashamed and cannot look up! He feels like an affectionate child or wife who has done something against the will of the parent or the husband.

The question naturally arises in every situation, will *this* or *that* please or displease him or her whom I love? Sinner, is this not true in your experience with respect to him or her who is the object of your greatest affection? Do you also, above all things, prize the approval of God? Does the consciousness of having done what He disapproves wring your heart with anguish, irrespective of its consequences to yourself? Do you feel the same emotions of sadness, shame, distress and sorrow when you have merited the disapproval of God that you do when you have offended your most beloved earthly friend? I appeal to your conscience. Do you not see that you do not supremely desire to please God?

The affectionate husband or wife, parent or child, is careful not to wound the feelings of those he loves. He has no rest until he has confessed and healed any wound he has caused. If you love God, you cannot consciously wound His feelings without pain. If you love God, you could not help repenting any more than an affectionate wife could refrain from grief if she had wounded her husband.

We Think About the People We Love

We naturally love to think of the one we love. Everyone knows how sweet it is to be alone, to meditate, to dwell upon some absent friend. Thus, lovers are apt to seek solitude, and there is a kind of sacredness thrown around those hours in the retirement of the lonely walk with delightful musings upon the person whom we love. These musings enkindle our affections into a flame.

See that husband who is traveling far away from home. He is a husband and a father. When the bustle of the day is over, when the distractions of business have passed away, see his busy thoughts going out and dwelling upon his absent wife and little children until his heart is all aglow and tears of unutterable affection fill his eyes. This is natural.

These laws of mind also apply when God is the object of supreme affection. The lone walk and the hour of sacred retirement are sweet to the Christian. He loves to think on God, to dwell upon His glories, to look into the mysteries of His love and to meditate on His glorious character over and over in his mind till his heart dissolves in love. Thus, the Psalmist says, "While I was musing, the fire burned." Now, sinner, do you love to think of God? Do you seek solitude that you may dwell upon Him. When you meditate and pray, do you find all-satisfying happiness? Do you have emotions of love to God as strong or stronger than those which you feel when thinking of your dearest earthly friend?

It gives us pleasure to speak of one we love. We enjoy speaking from the fullness of our hearts. This law of mind is just as true in religion as in any other subject. It is a maxim in philosophy, as well as in morals, that out of the abundance of the heart the mouth speaks.

Think of someone who loves God. If God is in all his thoughts, the interests of His kingdom will be in all his words. If his heart is set upon God, his lips will speak of God. If he is under circumstances where he cannot consistently speak of God, he is inclined not to speak at all. Sinner, do you love to converse about God? Is it delightful to you to speak of His character, of His person and of His glory? I leave it with your conscience to decide.

We hurt when separated from those we love. Everybody knows this is true with worldly friends; but it is true in a higher sense with respect to God. Every Christian knows what the saints of old knew, that they cannot live and have the least enjoyment if they are far from God. If He hides His face, if the manifestations of His presence are withdrawn, the Christian becomes lonely and sad, even in the midst of all the gaiety of the world around him. Sinner, have you ever felt pain at the withdrawal of God's presence?*

*See the wonderful sermons by Finney, "Joy in God," "The Benevolence of God," and "Revelation of God's Glory" in *Principles of Holiness*. These speak of the real joy of knowing God personally.

We Love the Friends of the People We Love

We naturally love the friends of the person we love, too. We feel attached to them for his sake. We love to converse with them and seek their company because their views of the person that engrosses our attention correspond with our own. Politicians who are in favor of the same candidate are fond of each other's company. Individuals, differing widely in other respects, enjoy each other's company if they have one common and absorbing object of conversation. Thus, Christians love to associate with one another. They love other Christians because they love God. They delight in their company, because their views and sentiments agree. But, sinner, do you love the friends of God? Do you love Christians *because they are Christians*? Do you delight in their conversation because they love God? You may love some of them for other reasons, and in spite of their religion, but it is not for their Christianity that you love them.

PRINCIPLE 27

REASON FROM EXPERIENCE

We naturally avoid the enemies of our friends. Would you find a woman running every day to spend time with enemies of her husband? Would she select friends from those who spoke against her husband and children? She instinctively avoids them. Imagine a little child. He goes to play with a neighbor child, but while playing, hears his friend's parents speaking against his father. He listens and grieves. He is little, and they do not notice him, but continue to abuse his father. He steals silently and sadly away and goes weeping home. Hereafter he will avoid those people as he would avoid a serpent. So with Christians; they naturally avoid those who abuse God, unless they mingle with them to warn and save them.

Sinners very often imagine that Christians avoid them because they think they are better. Some who profess to be Christians do not delight in the fellowship of the saints, but exhibit a preference for the company of the ungodly. This demonstrates that they are hypocrites. The law of mind still stands: "Know ye not, that the friendship of the world is enmity with God; he, therefore, who will be the friend of the world, is the enemy of God."

We are grieved when our beloved is abused in our presence. It is amazing to see the blindness and stupidity of sinners on this point. When Christians exhibit grief at the wicked conduct of sinners, sinners ascribe it all to superstition. If the pious father or mother exhibits grief when an unrepentant son or daughter is engaged in sin and rebellion against God, they imagine that it is all superstition and say, "They have forgotten that they were ever young."

Think of a husband who breaks the Sabbath and swears and abuses God. His wife weeps and leaves the room. He says his wife is very superstitious and is under the influence of witchcraft. He also wonders why she should worry about him when he can take care of himself. He does not seem to understand the principle upon which his wickedness affects her.

Suppose you are sitting in your house with your wife and someone comes in and begins to insult you in her presence. After he has said several vile things, he looks up and your wife is in tears. He asks, "What ails you, woman? You must be very superstitious. What affects you so?" What would you think of such questions? Would you not think it strange if he did not understand her tears? If your wife is a Christian and you disobey and abuse God in her presence, if she begins to weep, can you wonder about it and call it superstition?

Suppose your wife were to show no indignation when the man who entered your home began to insult you. Instead she appears pleased with it. You would not, you could not, believe that she loved you.

Christians Avoid Those Who Insult God

When God is abused in the presence of His friends, they feel grief and indignation. Naturally this is the reason why the company of unrepentant sinners is so disagreeable to a spiritual Christian. When Christians mingle with sinners, it is for business or for the purpose of doing them good, not because they have any delight in their unrepentant characters or conversation.

Sinner, are you grieved with those who disobey God? Does it pain you to hear a person swear in the streets, to see him break the Sabbath and trample on God's holy commandments? If you go through the streets and hear insults shouted about your dearest earthly friends, it would fill you with grief and indignation. If you pretend to love your Maker and you do not feel the same emotions when God is defamed, then you are a hardened and shameless hypocrite.

We are naturally pleased if we hear any good of one whom we love. It is a well-known fact that it is comparatively easy to believe what we desire to believe. A man will believe what he wants to, almost against testimony. He is not inclined to question the validity of the testimony by which the desired fact is established. We witness this law of mind at work every day, in religion as much as in any other area. When Christians hear of the conversion of anyone or of a remarkable revival of religion, they manifest a readiness to believe it because it accords with their desires. But do impenitent sinners show that they love God, that their hearts are set upon His glory and the interests of His kingdom? Do you manifest a readiness to believe what you hear in favor of Christianity? Let your conscience speak.

We love to see things used to make the ones we love happier. If we love an individual, we delight in those who honor him and try to promote his interests. We are not very particular about the way in which his pleasure is promoted, as long as it is successful. We naturally use the means that promise the highest success. Think of politicians. See how wise and energetic they are in devising and executing ways of electing their favorite candidate. You do not hear them stop to criticize any measure merely because it is new. If it is not wicked and if it promises success, its age has nothing to do with its being used.

Christians whose hearts are set on promoting the glory and honor of God are on the alert for new ways of achieving their favorite objective. They are consumed with the idea of bringing about the salvation of the world. But do sinners show that they are interested in the glory of God? Are you devising wonderful things for the Church? Are you finding new and more successful methods of promoting the glory of God and the salvation of men?

We Do Not Believe Evil About People We Love

It is difficult for us to believe an evil report of one whom we love. Go and tell some affectionate wife and mother of her husband's or son's disgraceful conduct. Do you find her ready to believe these reports? No, she will sift the testimony, criticize and scrutinize, and perhaps no weight of evidence can thoroughly convince her of the facts.

What lawyer has not tried to convince an unwilling juror? If a juror strongly desires not to believe the testimony of a witness, a slight inconsistency will be reason enough to disregard all the testimony. Report among warm-hearted Christians a story dishonoring to God and injurious to the interests of His kingdom. See how instantly they will ask for your authority, scrutinize and sift the testimony. You need not expect them to believe unless they see it.

Do sinners manifest this unwillingness to believe evil reports of God and His people? When they hear a scandalous report of any deacon, minister, or other professed child of God, do they instantly resist the report? Do they call for further proof? Do they sift and criticize the testimony as false and slanderous if they find discrepancy or absurdity in it? Do you feel indignation when a God-dishonoring report is circulated?

When an evil report about someone we love is proved true, we are careful not to give it unnecessary publicity. Does a mother go and publish the disgrace of her children? Does the affectionate wife trumpet the disgrace of her beloved husband? She locks it up in her faithful and affectionate bosom. So with Christians. Unless compelled by conscience to mention something harmful, it remains a secret. Are you careful not to circulate evil reports that you know to be true concerning God or His friends? If you hear anyone repeating something dishonorable to Christianity, does it distress you? Do you endeavor to hush the matter up and beg him not to repeat it? I leave the question with your conscience.

We naturally try to put the most favorable construction upon any event that might hurt the reputation of a friend whom we love. If something has occurred which we do not clearly understand, we naturally put the best possible construction upon it because that is most consistent with the honor of our friend. Love naturally hopes all things, believes all things, endures all things and is ever ready to put the most favorable construction upon any event that the nature of the case will admit. This principle operates in everyday occurrences. You will see Christians believing the thing most consistent with the honor of God. But do you witness this same disposition in sinners? Do you find in yourself a desire to construe every ambiguous occurrence in that way which is most favorable to Christianity? If a professor of religion says something wrong, do you naturally ascribe it to mistake or misunderstanding and find yourself very unwilling to believe that he meant to lie?

PRINCIPLE 28

KNOW IF YOU LOVE GOD

With all the facts from the preceding pages staring sinners in the face, how can they suppose they love God? Nothing is more common than for unrepentant sinners to say that they love God; and yet nothing is more certain than their lack of love for Him.

Sinners do not distinguish between an admiration of God's natural attributes and a love for His moral character. The omnipotence, omniscience, omnipresence, eternality and wisdom of God are attributes which are calculated to inspire awe in intelligent beings, whether they are sinful or holy. These attributes have no moral character. The devil himself may be filled with admiration when contemplating the displays of God's *natural* attributes, manifested throughout all creation.

Sinners mistake selfish gratitude for love to God. A supremely selfish being may be grateful for favors without any true regard for the character of the giver. Sometimes when sinners escape death by providence, they feel gratitude that they might feel toward Satan as easily as they do toward God, had he bestowed the same favor upon them.

Sinners Create Their Own God to Love

Sinners create their own god and fall in love with him. They think of God as they desire Him to be. They strip Him of His essential attributes and ascribe to Him a character that suits them, and then fall in love with their imaginary god, walk by the light of their own fire, and compass themselves with sparks of their own kindling. But present the *true* character of God and his heart becomes like the troubled ocean, which cannot rest, whose waters cast up mire and dirt.

Do you see why unrepentant sinners think Christianity is very gloomy? They have no love for God. What would you think of a woman who did not like to be with her husband? She complains of it as an irksome task. You would say it demonstrated that she did not love her husband. So it is with sinners. When they conceive of Christianity as something gloomy, something to rob them of all their joys, it shows that they do not love God; that they have no delight in pleasing Him.

Do you understand why sinners grow weary and complain of having too many long meetings? What would you think if you heard an individual who professed to love you complain of the time he had to spend with you? Could you believe that he loved you? When you hear sinners complaining that there are too many long meetings, is this not an index to their feelings? They do not love God. They have no delight in His services. It is a burden to them to be called to spend a short time in His presence.

Do you see why some who profess to be Christians prefer parties to prayer meetings? Prayer meetings are the most delightful parties for those who love God. But to those who do not love Him, they are not a source of happiness. They attend them from other motives than love for God. Whenever you see people who profess to be Christians exhibiting more interest in parties than in religious meetings, you may know they are hypocrites.

Everyone Needs a Change of Heart

Do you understand why sinners are deceived when they say they love God? There may be some people who were converted so young that they cannot remember the time when they did not love God. But they are very rare. Almost all of those who suppose they have always loved God are deceived. They have never had a change of heart. They feel toward God as they always have. If they ever *had* truly loved God, they would have discovered that it was something new to them.

Do you see why unrepentant sinners are often great hypocrites? They oppose hypocrisy and say that they like true religion. They claim to desire sincerity, to be good friends of God. But in professing such, they are blatant hypocrites. Christ would say to them, "I know you that you have not the love of God in you. Do people gather grapes from thorns, or figs from thistles? You justify yourselves before others, but God knows your hearts. You serpents, you generation of vipers, how can you escape the damnation of hell?"

Do you see the barefaced hypocrisy of those professing Christians who unnecessarily publish the faults of other Christians? We see them speaking with everyone about the real or supposed faults of the children of God. They will load down the winds with their complaints of the imprudence and errors of those closely associated with all the interests of religion. There is no just pretense that God requires this service at their hands. Sometimes they desire to publish these things in the newspapers, all under the sheer pretense of doing God service.

But this is the pretended motive of the Universalists in their slanderous publications against God and His servants. There is no reason to believe that they have the true interests of Christ's kingdom at heart. Professing Christians have entertained steamboat passengers and others in public places by telling slanderous reports of revival men. They have incited prejudice resulting in immense evils from this infidel conduct. Oh shame, where is thy blush!

"They Demonstrate That They Are Hypocrites"

If they truly loved the cause of Christ, it would be impossible for them to engage in this work of death, this mischief of hell, and to wantonly reproach the cause of Christ by spreading the real or imagined failings of those whose names and influence are identified with the dearest interests of the Church. They demonstrate that they are hypocrites as clearly as if they themselves should take their oath of it.

Sinner, if you think that you love God already, you will never realize that you need a change of heart. In pretending to love God, you deny the very foundation of the doctrine of the new birth. But, sinner, your delusion will soon be torn away. You cannot always deceive yourself. You are going rapidly into eternity. Even now, there is perhaps only a step between you and death. The moment that you appear in the presence of your Maker and behold the infinite difference there is between your character and His, your delusion will vanish forever. You pretend to love God, while you know that you have no delight in His Word or worship. Oh! What would heaven be to you if you cannot enjoy a prayer meeting; and what would you do in heaven employed in God's service forever. Would heaven be heaven to you? Would you feel at home? Away with this delusion: "For verily I say unto you, except a man be born again, he cannot see the kingdom of God."

PRINCIPLE 29

THE CARNAL MIND DOES NOT OBEY GOD

When the Apostle Paul wrote about the law of God in Romans 8:7, he was concerned about the the moral law, that law which requires people to love God with all their heart and their neighbor as themselves. He stated: "The carnal mind is enmity against God, for it is not subject to the law of God, neither indeed can be." The carnal mind does not obey God. While it continues to be hostile to God, it cannot obey the moral law. The Apostle affirms that a sinner cannot love God; for to say that a carnal mind can love God is the same as affirming that enmity itself can be love.

In the following pages, I will show what is not meant by the *carnal mind*, what *carnal mind* does mean, and that all who have not been born by the Spirit of God have a carnal mind. We must also see *how* this carnal mind is enmity against God.

When Paul wrote of the carnal mind, he did not refer to any part of the body. There is nothing in the body or mind that is opposed to God. The mind is not saturated with enmity. Carnal mind does not mean that the mind or body is so constructed that our nature is opposed to God. Nor does it mean that there are constitutional desires that are enmity against God.

To speak of the carnal mind does not mean that all the unconverted feel sensible emotions of hatred toward God. Enmity may exist in the mind either as volition or emotion. When existing in the form of *volition*, it is a settled *aversion* to His character and government. It is of such a nature that while it may have an abiding influence over our conduct, it may not have a *felt* existence in the mind.

Enmity Need Not Rise as Emotional Hate Toward God

When existing as an *emotion*, we become conscious of it and call it *feeling*. Enmity may be volitional, treating God as an enemy, without rising in conscious emotion. Specific emotions exist only when we think of those things that produce them. The primary reason why sinners do not frequently exercise emotions of hatred against God, and thus discover their enmity against Him, is because they seldom think of God. God is not primary in their thoughts. If they do think of Him, they do not think of Him as He really is. They deceive themselves with vain imaginations and hide His true character; thus they cover up their enmity.

The proper translation of *carnal mind* in this text is, *"the minding of the flesh."* It is a voluntary state of mind, that supreme selfishness in which all people are previous to their conversion to God.

The carnal mind is probably not a state of mind into which people are born, but into which they fall apparently very early after birth. People make the satisfaction of their desires the supreme object of pursuit, and this desire becomes the law of their lives, that law in their members that wars against the law of their minds.

They conform their lives and all their actions to this rule which they have established for themselves. It is nothing less than voluntary selfishness. Their rule of action is a preference for self-satisfaction beyond the commandments, and the authority and glory of God.

The Carnal Mind Is Voluntary Selfishness

Always remember that the carnal mind is not the mind itself, but a voluntary action of the mind. It is not a part of the mind or body, but a choice or preference of the mind. It is a *minding of the flesh*, preferring self-satisfaction before obedience to God.

The created desires of both body and mind are in themselves innocent, but making their satisfaction the supreme object of pursuit is enmity against God. It is the direct opposite of the character and the requirements of God. God requires us to subordinate all our desires to His glory, and to aim supremely at honoring and glorifying Him. God requires us to love Him with all our hearts, to bring all our powers of body and mind under obedience to the law of love. Whatever we do, whether we eat or drink, we should do all to the glory of God.

The minding of the flesh is the direct opposite of this. The carnal mind pursues as a supreme end the direct opposite of the requirements and character of God. It is a choice, a preference to glorify self.

Before conversion all people are in this state of enmity against God. The Bible speaks of people as possessing, by nature, one common heart. This text does not say that the carnal minds of some are enmity against God, but that *the carnal mind* is enmity against God. In another place, God says, "every imagination of the thoughts of their *heart* (not hearts), is only evil continually." Another passage says, "the *heart* of the sons of men is full of evil, and madness is in their *heart* while they live."

Throughout the Bible, unconverted people are spoken of as having a common heart. What the Bible asserts is seen to be a matter of fact. Go throughout the ranks of the human family, from the sensitive female that faints at the sight of blood to the horrid pirate whose eyes flash fire and whose lips burn with blasphemy; present to them all the claims of God and the gospel of His Son. They will plead their *inability*. Go to the refined and unrefined, to the learned and unlearned, to the high and low, rich and poor, old and young, male and female, bond and free of every country and not one of them can be persuaded to embrace the gospel. They will make *the excuse* that they cannot apart from the interposition of the Holy Spirit.

How is it possible to account for this notorious fact except upon this principle: that no matter how much the natural temperament may be made to differ in people (by education, by the state of the nervous system, or a variety of other considerations), they still possess the same disposition and will toward God. All, with one consent, begin to make excuses for not loving and obeying Him.

PRINCIPLE 30

THE CARNAL MIND IS HOSTILE TO GOD

The carnal mind, or minding of the flesh, is enmity against God. In earlier principles, I appealed to facts to demonstrate that unconverted people do not love God. Here I would like to establish that unrepentant sinners *positively hate* God. I appeal to the well-known laws of mind as we see them in everyday use.

We are naturally pleased with those things that our enemies hate. Whatever displeases our enemy satisfies our ill-will. It is the same as saying that the satisfaction of our desires pleases us. We witness the developments of this law of mind not only in our own case but in the feelings of those around us.

Even if some event has injured a person and he is a partaker in the common calamity, if it has much more deeply injured or ruined his bitter enemy, he considers it more than compensation for his own loss. He does not mind bearing the portion that has fallen to him, inasmuch as it has overwhelmed the man that he so deeply hates. Whatever he may say, his hatred is satisfied.

This same principle also develops toward God. Sinners manifest great pleasure in sin: it is the element in which they live and move. They drink up iniquity like water, even wearing themselves out sinning. They not only do these things, but have pleasure in others who do them. They love what God hates, and hate what God loves. They are against the character and will of God. The inclination of their minds is enmity against Him.

The Forsaking of an Enemy by His Friend Is Sweet

We are naturally gratified to see the friends of our enemy forsake and dishonor him. Suppose you hate another. If the children and friends of your enemy do anything to grieve, dishonor or injure him in any way, you may speak of it as if you were sorry, but it would be pure hypocricy. You rejoice in it because it gratifies your hatred.

You see this law of mind manifesting itself with equal uniformity and strength against God. When the professed friends of God forsake His cause and do anything to dishonor Him, unrepentant sinners are given great pleasure. They speak of it with exultation. While Christians converse about it with sorrow, weep over it, and pray that God will wipe away the reproach, it will become the song of the drunkard in barrooms and on streetcorners. They will laugh and rejoice.

An Enemy's Friends Are Searched for Faults

We are apt to magnify the faults of our enemy's friends. Politicians will scrutinize friends and supporters of an opposing candidate for any fault. They pay attention exclusively to their faults, forgetting that they have any virtues. Their faults appear so enormous that any appearance of virtue is ascribed to duplicity and hypocrisy. The man who is searching out all the failings of those that favor his enemy will be eagle-eyed.

This same spirit manifests itself toward God. Unconverted men fasten a malignant gaze on the professed friends of God. How eagerly they note their faults, enormously magnify them and ascribe every appearance of virtue to bigotry and hypocrisy.

We are likely to put the worst construction on the conduct of the friends of our enemies. If they favor the interests and endeavor to promote the happiness of one whom we greatly hate, we see all their conduct through a jaundiced eye. The best things in them are often ascribed by us to the worst of motives. Your acquaintance with your own heart will supply abundant proof of this remark.

This feature of the human character is often odiously developed toward God. We often hear sinners ascribing praise-worthy deeds of God's friends to the most unworthy motives. Only their enmity against God accounts for this. The people toward whom they direct their hate are often total strangers; individuals against whom they can have no personal hostility, except that they are friends of God. They manifest enmity only in that they resemble God; and this elicits hatred toward their cause and the Master whom they serve.

We naturally avoid the company of those who are particularly friendly to our enemy. Their company and conversation is irksome to us. This same spirit is manifest by impenitent sinners toward the friends of God. The presence of Christians seems to impose restraints upon sinners, and they cannot abuse God with quite as much freedom. They gladly avoid their company. In planning a party, impenitent sinners will arrange to exclude a minister or any other Christian from their company. This can only be accounted to their hate for God. They wish to avoid them because of the cause in which they are engaged and the Master whom they serve.

PRINCIPLE 31

SINNERS HATE TO THINK OF GOD

We naturally hate to think of our enemies. The human mind is distressed by malevolent emotions. Whenever our thoughts are intensely occupied in thinking of an individual whom we hate, malevolent emotions will naturally arise. These malevolent emotions cause us the misery of condemnation by the conscience. Therefore, unless we are planning revenge or in some way gratifying our hatred, we naturally turn our thoughts away from something we hate.

We naturally dwell upon pleasant things. Sinners banish God from their thoughts. They are "unwilling to retain God in their knowledge." If at any time the thought of God intrudes, they manifest uneasiness and immediately divert their attention.

However, if they are really convinced that they are sinners in danger of His wrath, their selfish regard for their own happiness may induce them to devise some means of escaping His just indignation.

We dislike talking about those whom we hate, unless it is to defame them. Unless we can pour forth our malignant hostility against them, we choose to remain silent. We love to visit about our friends because it expresses our love for them. It satisfies us. But even though there is pleasure in giving vent to our enmity in talking about our enemies, it is also the source of pain.

Have you witnessed the manifestations of this law of mind against Christianity? Sinners are averse to talking about God. They converse about Him reservedly, only in a manner that shows they have no pleasure in it.

Sinners Do Not Enjoy Hearing God Praised

We pain to hear our enemy praised. Imagine a party of friends in which the conversation turns to one well-liked fellow who is absent. They indulge themselves in enthusiastic commendations of their absent friend. But one sits embarrassed. He is secretly a bitter enemy of this friend of all. The rest, without heeding his agony, indulge themselves in praise for the one they love. The enemy looks at his watch, takes out his pipe, walks to the window, tries to read a newspaper, paces the floor and tries to introduce some other topic of conversation. But suppose that one of the ladies turns to him and asks his opinion, remarking that he seems to be distant and does not enjoy the conversation. If he is a gentleman, he may wish to waive an answer to her question. But suppose the group joins her and presses him for his opinion. One hundred to one, he will manifest the enmity of his heart.

How often sinners are offended! Go visit a family, some of whose members are Christians and others not. Sit down and visit warmly with the pious wife about the Christian faith in the presence of her unconverted family. What looks you will instantly perceive on other faces! Perhaps all will flee for the doors, and if any of the impenitent remain, turn and direct your conversation to one of them. The husband might forget that he is a gentleman and insult you to your face. Perhaps he will say that his religion is a matter between God and him, and that you are impertinent. Why does he consider you a disturbance? Certainly he has no reason to fear that you will injure him or his family. If he loved God, certainly he would thank you for your visit. Is it not proof that he hates God when he considers the subject an intrusion?

Sinners Hate to Hear of God's Success

We naturally detest hearing of the prosperity of our enemy. We are distressed to hear that he is gaining friends, popularity, property or influence. If there is any room for doubt, we are sure to question every point of the report.

Have you witnessed this principle with regard to Christian faith? Let a report of success in some great revival in the Church be circulated through the community, and see how Universalists and other sinners will manifest uneasiness and try to disprove it all. They will question the evidence. They do not believe that so many have been converted. "You will see," they argue, "that the professed converts will all go back again and be worse than ever. The reports are greatly exaggerated, and if there are any Christians in these revivals, there are probably ten hypocrites for every Christian." Such facts as these speak for themselves. They manifest a state of mind that cannot be mistaken. It is the boiling over of enmity against God.

PRINCIPLE 32

SINNERS HATE THE EFFORTS OF GOD

We naturally hate any efforts to promote the interests of our enemies. When we are opposed to the *end* which people have in view, then we are likely to object to their efforts. We will call their motives into question and find fault with their actions. We will ridicule their zeal and call it madness.

But think of sinners. If any effort is made to promote the interests of the kingdom of God, to honor and glorify Him, they are offended. They ridicule meetings and speak evil of those who are engaged in them, denouncing their zeal as mere madness.

Poor people may spend their time and money, waste their lives and health, and ruin their souls gambling and drinking; sinners may get together and dance all night, but no one objects. The nightclubs may be open every night, and the entertainers may prepare all day for the entertainment of the evening, but there are no complaints. The devil may set up long meetings like these and continue on for years, and sinners see no harm or madness in it. But let Christians exercise one-tenth of this zeal in promoting the honor of God and the salvation of souls and it would be condemned from Dan to Beersheba. For Christians to have late meetings, to pray till ten o'clock at night, is now abominable! Such activity becomes the subject of ridicule wherever impenitent sinners are assembled.

Politicians may be zealous for politics. They hold their caucuses, post their handbills, blaze away in the newspapers, parade through the streets with their music, show their flags and spend hundreds of thousands of dollars to carry an election; and no one thinks anything strange. But let Christians even begin to serve God with such zeal, making efforts to build up His kingdom and save the souls of men, and the wicked would absolutely mob them and cry out that such efforts would ruin the nation.

Is politics more important than the salvation of souls? Is effort wasted in arousing a slumbering world and bringing sinners to act, think, and feel as they ought on the subject of salvation? There is reason enough for any Christian effort, and sinners know it very well. But their hostility against God is so great that such efforts cannot be made without arousing all the hell there is within them.

Sinners Believe Any Evil Report About God

If a man hears any evil of an enemy, he believes it on the slightest testimony. He eagerly listens to every falsehood that serves to blacken the reputation of his enemy. His ill-will is gratified with such reports. He hopes that they are true and, therefore, easily believes them.

Sinners listen eagerly to every false and slanderous report that may be circulated about the friends of God. It is surprising to see what ridiculous things they will believe. Their hearts manifest hate to the degree that there is nothing too absurd and contradictory for them to believe.

We want others to share our hate. It gratifies our malignant feelings to hear and circulate reports about the enemy we hate. I hear people say to their neighbor, "Have you heard such and such a report about so and so? . . . Ah, I supposed that you knew it, or I would have said nothing about it." Hear him relate and aggravate every circumstance of which he has heard. After awhile he closes by saying, "I hope you will not mention this, but it is a fact." Soon he finds another ear and relates the same great secret. He is glad the event happened, and he delights to publish it. He covets the exclusive privilege of being the first bearer of the intelligence to every door.

We often witness this happening against God. If something disgraceful happens among the professed friends of God, sinners are ready to give it universal publicity. They will talk about it, blaze it abroad in the public press and send it in every direction upon the wings of the wind. If anyone becomes deranged in connection with a revival of religion, what a stir is made about it. Thirty thousand citizens of the United States may be murdered every year by strong drink. Liquor may fill asylums with maniacs. Homicide, suicide and other abominations may be the result of selling rum, and yet the indignation of sinners is not aroused. But if some individual becomes deranged in view of his abominable crimes against his Maker, the press groans with doleful complaints.

PRINCIPLE 33

SINNERS WOULD DESTROY GOD IF THEY COULD

Unrepentant sinners hate God with a *mortal hatred*. Were it in their power, they would destroy Him. Very few sinners probably realize that they have this degree of enmity against God; they may even be shocked at the assertion that they are this hostile against Him. Nevertheless, it is true.

There are several reasons why they may not know that this is the state of their hearts. Most of them have probably never dared to indulge in such thoughts and feelings. Even if they had the feelings, they never thought it possible to destroy Him.

Have you ever thought of being a king? You probably never did. You thought it was impossible. But suppose a throne, a crown and a sceptre were put within your reach. Suppose you were given the robe of royalty. Would you have the desire to be a king? After you had accepted the crown and swayed the sceptre over one nation, suppose you had the opportunity to extend your empire and make your dominion universal, ruling all the earth and the universe. Would you not do it? Accepting rule over God himself? *Sinners, who would trust the best among you?* If you suppose that under such circumstances there would be any limit to your ambition, then you do not know your own heart.

Sinners Are Unaware of Their Deep Enmity

Sinners do not realize the depth of their enmity against God. Because God presently lets them go unpunished, they do not believe that He will ever send them to hell for their sins. Their enmity remains relatively at rest. But who among them would not rise up and murder God were it in his power, if He attempted to punish them for their sins. Sinners would sooner see God in hell than consent that He should deal with them in justice.

Sinners are in rebellion against God, in league with devils to oppose His government and undermine His throne. They do everything that they can to annihilate His authority and destroy His government. Rebellion is always aimed at the life of the sovereign, and sinners want nothing less in their rebellion against God.

This whole issue has been proven. God once put himself in the power of men, as much as His nature would allow. The Son took a body. What was the result? Men did not rest until they had murdered Him. But you will argue that those were the Jews, that you are of a different spirit. This has always been the favorite plea of sinners.

The ancient Jews persecuted and murdered the prophets. The Jews of Christ's day professed to honor the prophets, so they built them sepulchres and insisted that if they had lived in the days of the prophets they would not have persecuted them. But they murdered Christ; and He himself informed them that by persecuting Him, they showed that they approved the deeds of their fathers.

Sinners Have Already Killed God

Suppose you lived in a monarchy. Your father had rebelled against the rightful king and placed a usurper upon the throne. You, as his child, although you did not participate in the original rebellion, now maintain the same ground which he took, supporting the usurper. Do you not become a partaker in your father's crimes, incurring the same guilt and deserving the same condemnation?

You did not murder Christ. But in refusing to obey Him as rightful sovereign, you support the authority of Satan (who has usurped the government of this world by refusing to repent) by withholding your heart from Jesus Christ. For all intents and purposes, you have become a partner in the crime. He claimed their obedience but they rose and stained their hands with His blood. He claims your obedience now, and you utterly refuse it. You prove by your disobedience, that rather than submit to His authority, you would murder Him again. You are guilty of the blood of Christ.

Sinners hate God *more than they do anything and everything else*. Do not be startled at this. It is the awful truth. All other enmity can be overcome by kindness. The greatest enemy you have on earth may win you as his friend with kindness. How is it that the infinite kindness of God has not overcome your enmity?

A mere change of circumstances in other cases of enmity will change the heart. Two political opponents, whose fathers were enemies, have always been enemies. They have both spoken evil of each other. But if a political change placed them on the same side, behind the same candidate, they would instantly become friends. They would cooperate and warmly shake hands. Their real feelings toward each other would be changed. They could say, "Whereas we formerly hated, now we love each other." All this has happened merely by a change of circumstances, without any interference by the Holy Spirit.

If the President of the United States appoints his greatest political opponent to the choicest office, he makes him his friend. Or suppose the greatest enemy of the President, who had said and done more than anyone to prevent his election, should be reduced to poverty. If the news reached the President and he appointed him to a post of high honor, would not this change his heart? Would he make the excuse that he *could not* become the President's friend until the Holy Spirit had changed his heart? Such kindness would be like pouring coals of fire upon his head; it would change the whole current of his soul.

Why then does it happen that with the offer of heaven and the threat of hell, with the boundless love manifested in giving

His well-beloved Son to die for you, with mercy stooping from heaven and reaching out with bleeding hands to offer salvation, and hell roaring from beneath and threatening to devour, that you make the excuse that these considerations will never change your heart, that the change must be effected by the Holy Spirit?

PRINCIPLE 34

SINNERS HATE TO THINK OF REPENTANCE

If people did not hate God so deeply, they would *instantly repent.* Suppose you were asleep in your home at midnight, and you were awakened by the cry of *fire.* You looked up and found your dwelling wrapped in flames. You leaped from your bed and found the floor ready to give way. The roof was beginning to collapse, ready to crash in upon you. Your little ones awoke and were shrieking and clinging to your night-clothes. You saw no way of escape. But suddenly someone came dashing through the flames, his hair and clothes singed black. He seized you with one hand and wrapped his other strong arm around your little ones before he rushed back through the flames. You swooned with terror. But in a few moments you opened your eyes and found yourself in the street, in the arms of your deliverer. He was wiping your face with water and fanning you to restore your fainting life. The scorched and smoky features hid the man whom you had supremely hated. He smiled and said, "Fear not, your children are all alive; they are all here." Could you look coldly at him and say, "Oh I wish I could repent that I have hated you so much. I wish I could be sorry for my sin against you"? Could you say this? This event would change your heart. If you heard him slandered, it would kindle your grief and indignation.

How can you complain that you *cannot* repent of your sins

against God? Behold His lovingkindness and His tender mercy. How can you refrain from repentance? Behold His bleeding hands! See His wounded side! Hear His deep death-groan, "It is finished," when He yields up His spirit for your sins. Are you marble or granite? Has your heart been so case-hardened in the fires of hell that you won't repent? Nothing but enmity deep as perdition could withstand the call.

The Age of Mercy Is Now

But perhaps you do not like to hear about hell and damnation, only love and mercy. If ministers would present God as loving and merciful, then you would love Him. But what are those cries of *Crucify him! Crucify him!* that break upon our ears over more than 1800 years? God *has* revealed His mercy, and the world still rises up against it. Jesus Christ came on the errand of salvation, and the world filled with uproar to murder Him. Mercy is the very attribute of God against which mankind is arrayed. For hundreds of years, the sword of justice has slept in the scabbard, and God has been holding out His attribute of mercy.

What is Christianity? The Bible? Revivals? They are exhibitions of the mercy of God. Justice will soon hush the loud opposition of sinners against their Maker. Every mouth shall be stopped and all the world shall be found guilty before God. But we are still under His mercy, and all the earth is up in arms against it. Why are you such a hypocrite as to pretend to love the mercy of God? If you love it, why not accept it? Do not say you love any attribute of God, for you are a liar and the truth is not in you.

Do you see why Universalists are so disturbed with revival? They cannot bear such an exhibition of God's mercy. It disturbs all the lurking enmity of their hearts. As soon as God displays himself and men become the recipients of His mercy, these professed friends of God are greatly offended.

We Must Preach Man's Enmity Against God

Do you see the importance of preaching clearly and frequently about how sinners hate God. There is, and always has been, a weakness in presenting this important subject. Ministers seem to be afraid to tell people that they are the enemies of God. Previous to my own conversion, I never heard this doctrine declared in a way that I understood it. Many ministers seemed to regard total depravity as nothing more than the *absence* of love for God.

The Church does not seem to have realized or believed that *the carnal mind is absolute enmity against God*. Although there is no other truth more thoroughly presented in the Word of God, few sinners have been made to see and believe it. In hundreds of instances, I have conversed with people who have sat under the preaching of the gospel all their days, and who had never heard this fundamental truth of the gospel.

Man's enmity against God is the foundation of the need for new birth. We cannot expect the world to be converted without understanding and believing that.

Even if sinners would take an oath that they hate God, it could not be any clearer that they do. If everyone in the universe were to swear that the sun shines at noon, it would not change the evidence that it does. It is a fact proven by our own senses. Sinners constantly act out their rebellion against God. How their enmity ever came to be overlooked is most mysterious.

There are many professors of religion who could not make it more evident that they are the enemies of God even if they would swear to it. They speak against revivals and those engaged in promoting them. They speak of the faults, real or imagined, of the friends of God. They retail slander and oppose God in so many ways that their enmity against God is perfectly obvious.

PRINCIPLE 35

SINNERS MUST ADMIT THEIR ENMITY AGAINST GOD

Sinners who have not understood that they are enemies of God have been neither converted nor convicted. What have they repented of? Repentance is impossible, unless they have understood and condemned the fountain of iniquity from which their abominations have proceeded. The core of their offenses is that they have been the enemies of God. They talk of having repented when they have never known this. Impossible!

Those who deny they are enemies of God will never be converted until they confess their enmity. "He that covereth his sins, shall not prosper, but whoso confesseth and forsaketh them, shall have mercy." There are many who will confess themselves sinners but deny that they are the enemies of God. Thus they cover up the enormity of their sins and acknowledge only their outward acts of wickedness, but deny the enmity from which they flow.

I am presenting a very different view of total depravity than those who regard it as physical. Depravity is *voluntary* transgression, the sinner's own act, that over which he has perfect control and for which he is entirely responsible. There is confusion in saying that depravity is transmitted from Adam, something hidden, some physical pollution which is sinful and deserving the wrath of God previous to the exercise of voluntary agency. This is absurd.

Sinners Must Repent of Their Enmity

Sinners virtually blame God for all sin. Repentance becomes a natural impossibility. While the sinner supposes himself condemned for his nature, it is impossible for him to blame himself for his sins. He must cease being reasonable. No wonder people who maintain this view of depravity also maintain that sinners are *unable* to repent. The only way in which God can bring a sinner to repentance is by correcting his views; by showing him that he must repent of sinful conduct and not sinful nature. To teach physical depravity is to teach heresy, leading sinners inevitably to justify themselves and condemn God.

Do you see why sinners find it so hard to become Christians? They are unwilling to yield up their selfishness.

No one can logically claim that I am denying *moral* depravity. I have purposely spoken against physical depravity. It is moral depravity for which the sinner is to blame, that of which he must repent.*

Some assume that denying the depraved sinful nature is a virtual denial of all depravity. They think it a denial of the *guilty source* of transgression. But the settled preference of a sinner's soul, the choice of self-satisfaction over the will of his Maker, constitutes the deep fountain from which the putrid waters of spiritual and eternal death flow. I do not understand how *moral* depravity is derived from physical *natural* depravity. Why call it *moral* depravity? Certainly it would have no relation to moral law and its just punishment. I am surprised that in the nineteenth century it is considered heresy to insist that sin must be a voluntary *act*. What next? Certainly Paul was not orthodox, if sin is not a voluntary act.

It is plain that sinners must be annihilated, converted or forever lost. With a mind that is at enmity with God, it is naturally impossible for them to be happy. Total depravity is abundantly manifest as a fact, even without the testimony of the Bible. But the Bible presents a change of heart, the new birth,

---

*See *Finney's Systematic Theology* for his careful distinction between moral depravity and physical depravity. Finney believed both terms must be carefully defined to avoid the confusion so prevalent in his day as well as our own.

which delivers sinners from their depravity, from their sinfulness.

Sinners Are Closer to Hell Than Heaven

Sinners are not *almost* Christians, as people sometimes describe them. The most moral sinner is much nearer a devil than a Christian. He need only die to be in hell. He needs no positive influence to become a fiend; just remove all restraints and the enmity of hell boils over in his heart. Let God remove His supporting hand for a moment and he would open his eyes in eternity, and curse Him to His face.

It would be impossible for sinners to enjoy heaven. If they were pushed into the presence of God to behold His glories, see holiness to the Lord inscribed on everything around them and hear the song of "Holy, holy, holy, Lord God Almighty," their enmity would be so great that they would dive into the darkest cavern of hell, if they could, just to escape the presence of the infinitely holy Lord God.

While sinners remain unrepentant, they yield no more obedience to God than the devil does. Until the supreme preference of their mind is changed, until they have given up minding the flesh and begin to obey God, it is vain to talk of obedience. The first act of obedience that you can perform is to cease minding the flesh and give your heart to God.

Do you see the folly of parents who think their unconverted children are not enemies of Christianity. No wonder their children are not converted. It is just what the devil desires the children to hear. If they assume that they already have goodwill for Christianity, they cannot be convicted, no less converted.

Do you see the falsehood of saying of an impenitent sinner that he is a good-hearted man? The fact is that his heart has enmity against God.

Do you see how necessary hell is? What shall be done with these enemies of God if they die in their sins. Heaven is no place for sinners. It would be worse than being in hell. Hell is necessary for those who die in enmity against God. Do you see your state? Your enmity is voluntary. It is your own creation;

that which you have long cherished and exercised. Will you give it up? What has God done that you should continue to hate Him? What is there in sin that you should prefer it to God? Why will you indulge, for a moment longer, this spirit of horrible rebellion and enmity against God? A little further and the knell of eternal death shall toll over your damned soul, and all the corners of despair will echo with your groans.

PART 5

Why Sinners Hate God

"They have hated me without a cause"
(John 15:25).

PRINCIPLE 36

KNOW WHY SINNERS HATE GOD

Our Lord Jesus Christ said: "They have hated me without a cause" (John 15:25). In Part 4 on *Total Depravity*, we have seen that unrepentant sinners hate God above everything else. It is now important to discover *why sinners hate God*. In this part, I will show the reason for their hatred and that they hate God for the very reasons for which they ought to love Him.

If sinners have good reason for hating God, then they are not to blame for it; but if not, or if they hate Him when they ought to love Him, they are guilty for their enmity against God.

The reason for their hatred is not because God has created them with a physical aversion to God. The text affirms that sinners have hated God without cause. Not that there is no reason why they hate Him, but no *good* reason, for every effect must have some cause. If God had incorporated aversion to himself in the sinner, this would be a sufficient cause; not only for the sinner's hating Him, but a good reason why all other beings should hate Him.

The sinner's enmity is not caused by a transmitted *disposition* to hate God. *Disposition* is an action of the mind, not a part of the mind itself. Therefore, it is absurd to talk of an hereditary *disposition* to love or hate God or anything else. It is impossible for a *voluntary* state of mind to be transmitted from one generation to another.

If someone defines *disposition* as a propensity which is not

158

a voluntary state of mind but an attribute that is not actually part of the mind, I would have to say that the sinner's hatred is not caused by anything which influences the mind.

There Is No Physical Reason for Enmity

There is no just cause in our physical nature for opposition to God. The nature of man is as it should be. Its powers are as God made them. He has made them perfectly, just as we could expect infinite power, goodness and wisdom to make them. They are perfectly adapted to serving the Creator. If we study the delicate organization of the body and scrutinize the powers and capacities of the mind, we find no just cause to complain, but rather infinite reason to love and adore the great architect, and exclaim with the Psalmist, "I am fearfully and wonderfully made."

There is no just cause for the sinner's hatred, considering the wise and loving arrangement by which all people have descended from one common ancestor. By divine arrangement, it is natural (*not necessary*) for our characters to be modified by those with whom we grow up. We naturally influence each other and modify each other's character. But like every other good thing, this arrangement can be abused. Our influence to promote virtue when we do *right* is great, but our potential to promote vice is just as strong, if we do *wrong*.

There is no cause for the sinner's hatred. God's commandments are easily obeyed, and obedience naturally results in happiness; "His yoke is easy, and His burden is light." If God had established requirements so high that they were extremely difficult to fulfill or if the laws were so intricate and difficult to understand that an honest mind would be in great danger of mistaking their real meaning, sinners would have just cause to hate God. But God designed the perfect government.

There Is No Excuse in the Gospel for Enmity

Sinners have no just cause for hating the requirements of the gospel. If the conditions of salvation were arbitrary or unjust, if it were impossible for humans to comply with them, if God commanded repentance when they had no power to repent, or if He required them to believe when they had no power to believe, sinners would have reason to hate God. But none of these conditions are true. The demands of the gospel are far from arbitrary. They are imperative to the nature of salvation. They are made as simple as possible, without rendering salvation impossible. Repentance and faith are indispensable for preparing the soul for the enjoyment of heaven. If God dispensed with these conditions and the sinner remained in his sins, it would render the sinner's damnation certain.

Not only are the conditions of salvation necessary, but they are easier to comply with than to reject them. Our minds are as well suited to accept as to reject the gospel. But the motivation to accept the offers of mercy is infinitely greater than to reject. The motivation is so strong that sinners often find it difficult to resist, and they must make almost ceaseless efforts to maintain themselves in unrepentance and unbelief.

God's Providential Government Is Perfectly Administered

There is no reason to doubt that God administers His providence, His providential government, to produce the highest possible influence in favor of holiness. Everything possible has been done to secure universal holiness.

God's providential government is doubtless administered solely for the benefit of *moral* government. Many sinners talk as if they supposed that God might more justly administer His government, both moral and providential, to secure the perfect moral conduct of His subjects. They seem to think that because God is almighty, He can secure perfection in moral agents. Sin in our world, therefore, would be conclusive proof that He prefers sin to holiness, even though He sometimes opposes sin. This is a most wicked assumption. It is not a fair inference from the omnipotence and omniscience of God.

God's character is no ground for hate. There is no inconsistency between His conduct and His professions. Some people have conceived of God as a sly, hypocritical being, who says one thing and means another; who professes abhorrence of sin, yet conducts the affairs of His kingdom to purposely produce sin. They say He commands men to keep His law or face eternal death, but prefers that they break it; He commands all to repent and believe the gospel, yet has made atonement only for the elect, who are so created that He knows they are unable to repent. All these claims are a libel upon His infinitely upright conduct.

There is nothing unkind or overly severe in the conduct of God toward mankind. Sinners have often complained of His unjust dealings, sometimes wondering what they had done to receive His severe chastisement. But the conduct of God places Him above suspicion.

PRINCIPLE 37

KNOW HOW HATRED OF GOD BEGINS

Sinners hate God because they are supremely selfish. God, as He ought to be, is infinitely opposed to their supreme object of pursuit. The first thing that we discover about little children is their desire for self-satisfaction. It is impossible for us to say when this desire becomes selfishness. There is nothing sinful about satisfying a desire for food and drink or any other desire in a proper way. These desires have no moral character and satisfying them properly is not sinful. But whenever we overstep the laws of God in fulfilling them and allow the desire to command our actions, we sin. We make our own desire the rule of duty, instead of following the requirement of God. We indulge ourselves rather than follow the highest good for everyone. This is the essence and the history of sin.

We probably cannot remember when we first made self-satisfaction the supreme object of choice. Our depravity commenced at that moment. It was our first moral act. Everything that had preceded this had no moral character at all. The Bible assures us that this occurs so early in our history that it may be said that "the wicked are estranged from the womb. That they go astray as soon as they are born, speaking lies." This language is not to be understood literally. After all, we do not speak as soon as we are born. But the wicked speak lies as soon as they do speak: when they are very young. "Behold," says the Psalmist, "I was shapen in iniquity, and in sin did my mother conceive me." Certainly this language is also figurative, for it cannot be possible that a fetus is sin, that it has sinful components! This would contradict God's own definition of sin. God says, "Sin is a transgression of the law," and the law prescribes a rule of action, not a mode of existence. If a fetus is sin, then the sin is God's. The only way to understand these passages, without making utter nonsense of the Word of God, is to see that they refer to the commencement of our moral existence—from the earliest moment of the exercise of moral agency. Insist that these passages are literal and you will prove not only that sin and holiness are substances, but that God is a material being.

The Great Error of Depravity

The great error on the subject of depravity is this: the rule of interpretation that all language is to be understood according to the nature of the subject to which it is applied has been overlooked, and the one meaning has been attached to one word, whether applied to matter or to mind. For instance, to set aside God's definition of sin (*a transgression of law*), and to literally read these figurative expressions that would seem to represent sin as something other than voluntary transgression is to array Scripture against itself. It is to tamper with the Word of God. It is tempting the Holy Spirit. It is a stupid, not to mention willful, perversion of the truth of God.

The great reason sinners are opposed to God is not that there is a defect in their nature forcing them to oppose Him, but because God is irreconcilably opposed to their selfishness. He is opposed to the supreme end of their pursuit, to their obtaining happiness in a way that is inconsistent with His glory and the happiness of all other people.

The sinner's supreme aim is the promotion of his own happiness. It is inconsistent with the public good. With an unholy end in view, the means he uses are just as wicked. God is therefore opposed to the means just as much as He opposes the end which he is endeavoring to accomplish. These means are his sins, making up the history of his life. They are all designed, directly or indirectly, to affect the all-absorbing goal, the promotion of his own happiness.

God is, therefore, conscientiously opposed to everything which sinners do or say while they are unrepentant. They would place everything at the mercy of their own interests. But God insists that they seek their happiness consistent with the happiness of the whole. This is, after all, the only way in which they can be happy. He therefore attempts to defeat everything they do to obtain happiness in their own way. He is the irreconcilable adversary of all their selfish schemes. He embitters every cup of selfish joy.

Sinners Hate God for His Holiness

Thus you see that sinners hate God because He is holy. While they remain sinners, their characters, their desires and all their ways are diametrically opposed to His ways. Until they change, God says, "I loathe them, and they abhor me."

Holiness is trying to do right. God requires, upon infinite penalties, that every moral being do and say that which is perfectly right. He cannot require less without injustice. But sinners are unwilling. Of course they consider God an enemy, because He insists upon their unqualified obedience to the law of right. He stands in the way of all their selfish schemes.

Sinners hate God because He is so good. He is good and does good, and promotes the public interest in a way that often overturns their selfish Babel towers. His heart is so set upon doing good that He has overthrown families and nations that stood in His way. He once flooded the world of sinners to prevent their mischief, that through the law and gospel, He might reclaim mankind and save a multitude from hell.

Sinners hate God because He is impartial. They view their own interest as most important. Thus they arrange their lives to allow the universe to perpetuate their own happiness. But since God has an entirely different end in view, He continually thwarts their favorite projects. The universe is arranged and governed to make shipwreck of their fondest hopes.

But this is not all. Sinners hate God because He threatens

to punish them for their sins. He will not compromise with them. He requires their repentance and reformation, or the everlasting destruction of their souls. Either alternative is detestable to the impenitent sinner. To repent, to heartily confess that God is right and he is wrong and to take God's side against himself, to dedicate himself with all he is and has to the service of God and the promotion of the public interest is what he is utterly unwilling to do. God insists upon it. The sinner, therefore, considers God as his infinite and almighty adversary and makes war upon Him with all his heart.

PRINCIPLE 38

GOD'S LOVE CAN INSPIRE HATRED

Sinners hate God for the very reasons for which they ought to love Him: God opposes sin and injurious conduct of every kind because He highly regards individual and general happiness. These are the incentives for reasonable beings to love their Maker; because He deserves to be loved. It is for these very reasons that sinners hate Him. They hate Him because He deserves their love and because He is good. They have no reasonable motive to hate Him, but every possible reason to love Him.

Man's Enmity Does Not Rise from His Nature

The wicked actions of sinners are no proof that their nature is sinful. The universal sinfulness of man has been inferred as proof that the nature of man must be sinful. Some assume that there is no other way to account for the universally sinful conduct of man. They maintain that an effect must be of the same nature as its cause; and since our actions are sinful, our nature must also be sinful.

We can see the absurdity of this argument by using an analogy. If the effect must be of the same nature as its cause, then God must be a material being because He is the cause of the material universe. By analogy, the soul of man must be material because it acts upon his material body. Following this line of reasoning, we can dispose of all spirits, for they all act on the material world. This argument is meaningless.

The sinful conduct of all men is easily accounted for by the principles laid down in the previous pages. When people adopt the principle of selfishness as their great rule of action, this takes over and gives a sinful character to every moral action.

Some may ask why all children adopt the principle of self-ishness without a sinful nature. They practice selfishness because they possess *human nature* and because they enter a fallen world, surrounded by temptation.

All the desires of body and mind are *in themselves innocent*, but they can be strongly excited by powerful temptations to prohibited satisfaction. So many temptations are made to these natural desires that all human beings are led to sin. Adam was created in the perfection of manhood, certainly not with a sinful nature; and yet, an appeal to fulfill his innocent desires in a sinful way brought him into sin. If adult Adam, without a sinful nature, even after a period of perfect obedience, was led to change his mind by an appeal to his innocent desires, then we can see how infants with the same human nature, but surrounded by still greater temptation, so quickly fall into sin. This does not mean that their nature is sinful. It is absurd to maintain that the infant's choice to sin is proof of the sinful nature; but even more incredible is the belief that sin is a part of the body instead of voluntary action. This is impossible!

The inference of a "sinful nature" is particularly evil because in making it we reject God's own declaration that "sin is a transgression of the law." Instead we adopt a definition which is perfectly absurd. From the view of depravity presented in these principles, it is easy to see in what sense sin is natural to sinners; and what has led mankind to ascribe sin to their nature.

Our Supreme Preference Rules Our Actions

Our experience shows that the supreme preference of our minds influences our conduct directly or indirectly. When we desire a thing supremely, it is *natural* for us to pursue it. We may have desires for things which we do not pursue, but it is senseless to say that we do not pursue our supreme desire. It is the controlling choice, driving the will which controls our actions. Because sinners adopt the principle of supreme selfishness, it is natural for them to sin; obedience is impossible. This is why "the carnal mind is not subject to the law of God, neither indeed can be."

Because all men sin, mankind has ascribed the sins of men to their nature. We blame nature, but actually *sin is an abuse of the powers of nature*. People have overlooked the deep-seated, but voluntary, preference for sin as the fountain of all other sins. The only sense in which sin is natural to people is that they naturally are controlled by their supreme choice. It will, therefore, always be natural for a sinner to sin, until he changes the supreme preference of his mind to glorify God and the interests of His kingdom.

PRINCIPLE 39

SALVATION IS BY GRACE

Perhaps someone will object, "If infants are not born with a sinful nature, how can they be saved by grace?" But if they *are* born with a sinful nature, how can it be called *grace* to save them? Does God create a sinner and then call it grace to save the infant from the very nature of His own creation? Absurd and blasphemous. Can we present God as either directly or indirectly creating a sinful nature?

There are two schools of thought. One maintains that infants have no moral character at all before they sin. Their first moral actions are invariably sinful, but previous to moral action they are neither sinful nor holy. Since they have no moral character, they deserve neither praise nor blame; neither life nor death at the hand of God. God might annihilate them without injustice, or He might give them eternal life as a free and unearned gift.

The other school declares that infants have a sinful nature inherited from Adam. The Scriptures say that any man ever saved must be saved by grace. Therefore, this school holds that only in their system is it possible to ascribe the salvation of infants who die before actual transgression to grace.

Let us examine these systems. We generally refer to grace as *unmerited favor*. But sometimes it also carries the broader idea of mercy or forgiveness. When infants die previous to actual transgression, it is impossible to ascribe their salvation to

169

grace in any other sense than unearned favor. If they have never sinned, we cannot include the idea of mercy or forgiveness. The child cannot be *pardoned* for having a sinful nature. But neither has he ever earned eternal life, never having done anything to deserve it. God might annihilate him without injustice. But since it pleases Him for the sake of Christ to give eternal life, He grants it in grace.

Infants Live by God's Grace

I deny that infants have a sinful nature. God has not created the nature sinful merely to pretend to save the infant from a nature of His own creation. The very existence of mankind is a matter of grace based on the atonement of Jesus Christ. Had it not been for the anticipated atonement, Adam and Eve would have been sent to hell at once; *mankind* would never have existed. Adam and Eve would have been the last humans had it not been for the grace of Christ in interposing on behalf of them by His atonement.

Every infant owes its existence to the grace of God in Jesus Christ. If it dies before actual transgression, it is just as indebted to Christ for eternal life as if it had been the greatest sinner on earth.

Neither of these schemes includes the idea of pardon in the grace accorded to infants. Nevertheless, both schools attribute the existence of mankind to the atonement, and both recognize that the infant is delivered from temptation under which it would certainly have earned eternal death. Therefore, to claim that the view of depravity I have given denies the grace of God in the salvation of infants is to either misunderstand or willfully misrepresent my sentiments.

Is there more grace displayed in the salvation of infants through either school of thought? It might be said that in neither case does the infant need a pardon, yet in one case his nature must be changed, and not in the other. I deny that changing the infant's nature is an act of grace. If God made his nature incapable of performing any but sinful actions, He is required to change it. It is silly to call this grace.

Sinners Hate God's Grace

The hatred of sinners is cruel. It is, as God says, "Rendering hatred for his love." God is love, and this is the only reason why they hate Him; not because they overlook the fact that He is infinitely benevolent. They render hatred for His love. He desires their happiness and opposes their making themselves miserable. More than any earthly parent, He wants to keep His child from anything that will injure him. He pleads with sinners, "Oh, do not that abominable thing that I hate." "How shall I give thee up Ephraim? How shall I deliver thee Israel? How shall I make thee as Admah? How shall I set thee as Zeboim? My heart is turned within me, and my repentings are kindled together."

As children sometimes hate and revile their parents for opposing their wayward courses to destruction, so sinners hate God more than they hate all others, because He is infinitely opposed to their destroying their own souls. The better God is, the more they hate Him; for the better He is, the more He opposes their selfishness.

The Sinner Is Guilty Because He Rejects Grace

In my principles regarding depravity, I showed that sinners hate God above everyone else because of His supreme excellence. His goodness is unmingled goodness, therefore their hatred is unmingled enmity. If there were any defect in His character, people would not hate Him so much. If God were not perfectly good, people might not be totally depraved, they might not be totally opposed to His character.

The more He tries to do sinners good, the more they will hate Him. While they retain their selfishness, His efforts to hedge them in, to prevent the accomplishment of their selfish desires, to tear away their idols and to wean them from the world, the more He embitters every cup of joy with which they attempt to satisfy themselves.

The sinner is accountable for this conduct and deserves eternal death. It is impossible to conceive of guilt deeper than that of sinners rejecting the gospel. Even demons have never rejected the gospel, never spurned the offer of eternal life through the atoning blood of the Son of God. If sinners do not deserve hell, I do not believe that there is a demon in hell that deserves it. And yet sinners often speak as if it were doubtful whether they deserve to be damned.

Saints and angels will be entirely satisfied with the justice of God in the damnation of sinners. They will never take delight in the misery of the damned, but in the display of justice, in the vindication of His insulted majesty and injured honor. They will cry hallelujah, while "the smoke of their torment shall ascend forever and ever."

PART 6

God Cannot Please Sinners

"And the Lord said, Whereunto, then, shall I liken the men of this generation? And to what are they like? They are like unto children sitting in the market-place, and calling one to another, and saying, We have piped unto you, and ye have not danced; we have mourned to you, and ye have not wept. For John the Baptist came neither eating bread nor drinking wine, and ye say he hath a devil! The Son of Man is come eating and drinking, and ye say, Behold a man is come eating and drinking, and ye say, Behold a gluttonous man and a wine-bibber, a friend of publicans and sinners! But wisdom is justified of all her children" (Luke 7:31–35).

PRINCIPLE 40

GOD'S LAW CANNOT PLEASE SINNERS

John the Baptist was an ascetic. He seems to have had very little fellowship with the public except as a prophet. His message carried severe rebuke. He ate locusts and wild honey, and seems to have practiced austerity in all his habits. He did not visit Jerusalem as a public teacher, but stayed in the wildest parts of Judea where the people flocked to listen to his instructions. His habits of life, his style of preaching and his asceticism led his enemies to say that he was not a good man, but that he was possessed with the devil.

After the scribes and Pharisees had rejected John's doctrine under the pretense that he had a devil, Jesus Christ began His public ministry. His lifestyle differed widely from John the Baptist. Instead of confining himself to the wilderness of Judea, He visited most of the principal cities and spent considerable time at Jerusalem as a public teacher. He was affable, mingling with great ease and holy politeness with all classes for the purpose of instructing in salvation. He did not hesitate to accept the dinner invitations of the Pharisees and other great men of the nation; but on all occasions administered suitable reproof and instruction.

But when the Pharisees listened to Him, they became angry with the way He rubbed shoulders with and instructed all classes of people. They called Him a gluttonous man, a winebibber, a friend of publicans and sinners. They had objected to

John as morose and sour. But they objected that Christ was on the opposite extreme, too affable and too familiar with all classes of people. It was this inconsistency in them that drew forth from Christ the words of our text.

"You would not dance"

An allusion is made in the text to Eastern customs, to their festivities and dances and to their loud funeral lamentations. It is common for little children to copy those things which they see in adults. When they witness piping and dancing at festivals, they get something that will serve as an instrument and they go forth piping and dancing in imitation of what they have seen.

The behavior of the scribes and Pharisees is compared to children who sit in the market-place and complain of their little playmates as morose and sour, unwilling to play the games they want to play. When they imitated festivity, their playmates were solemn. But when they played something more agreeable to their sullen mood and wailed unto them as if at a funeral, they were merry. *We have piped unto you and ye have not danced; we have mourned to you, and ye have not wept.* When Christ had thus represented the testy conduct of these children, He pressed home the application, "For John the Baptist came neither eating bread, nor drinking wine, and ye say he hath a devil. The Son of Man is come, eating and drinking, and ye say, Behold a gluttonous man, a wine-bibber, a friend of publicans and sinners! But wisdom is justified of all her children."

God's Character Does Not Please Sinners

God cannot please sinners. Some people imagine that it is a misrepresentation of God's character which creates so much opposition to Him. Sometimes His character is greatly misrepresented; and men's *consciences* oppose Him. But they are no better pleased when His character is truly represented, for then their *hearts* are opposed to Him.

We need not prove that the heart and the conscience of unrepentant sinners are opposed to each other. That which their hearts love, their consciences condemn, and vice versa. Their consciences approve the character of God, but their hearts are utterly opposed. (I have shown this when treating the subject of total depravity.) If the character of God could be altered to please their wicked *heart*, their *conscience* would condemn it.

Sinners do not like the holiness of God, nor would they like Him if He were unholy. To maintain that an unrepentant heart loves holiness is the same as saying that it is not unrepentant; for unrepentance loves sin. Opposites are not alike. God is infinitely holy, therefore the unrepentant heart is *wholly* opposed to Him. Imagine He were infinitely sinful. Would sinners be better pleased with Him than they are at present? They would then war against Him because He was so wicked. Their consciences would then condemn Him, and although their hearts would be conciliated, their better judgment would utterly oppose Him.

People are so made that they cannot approve the character of a wicked being. No one ever appreciated the character of the devil. Wicked people are opposed to both God and the devil, for opposite reasons. They hate God with their *hearts* because He is so *holy*; and their *consciences* condemn the devil because He is so *wicked*.

Imagine placing the character of God at any point between the two extremes of infinite holiness and infinite sinfulness. Sinners would be no better pleased with Him than they are now. Their hearts would hate Him to the degree of His holiness, and their consciences would condemn Him to the degree of His wickedness. He does not please them as He is, nor would He please them if He should change.

God's Motives for Righteousness Do Not Please Sinners

There is scarcely anything in the character of God more revolting to an unrepentant heart than the awful justice that threatens sinners with eternal death. But if He were unjust, their consciences would condemn Him.

Neither do sinners like the mercy of God, nor would they

like Him if He were unmerciful. If they appreciated His mercy with its conditions, they would accept forgiveness.

Sinners do not like God's law as it is, nor would they approve if it were altered. When they understand its perfection, their hearts rise up against it. But if it were imperfect and allowed some degree of sin, their consciences would condemn it. The law requires perfect holiness, and for this reason the sinner's heart is entirely opposed to it.

Sinners do not like the penalty of the law, nor would they approve of it if it were altered. The hearts of sinners rise into outrageous rebellion when the penalty of eternal death is displayed. But if the penalty were less, their consciences would say the penalty was not equal to the importance of the precept. Unless the penalty were eternal death, they would say God had not done everything necessary to prevent sin.

PRINCIPLE 41

GOD'S GOSPEL CANNOT PLEASE SINNERS

Sinners do not like the gospel as it is, nor would they be satisfied if it were altered. They do not like the *rule of conduct* it prescribes. The gospel requires that we be holy, as God is holy. It requires the same strictness as the moral law. But this offends the sinner's *hearts*. Suppose it prescribed a lesser rule of conduct to suit our sinful inclinations, then their *consciences* would oppose it.

"What?" they would say. "Is the gospel to repeal the moral law? Does it make Christ the minister of sin? Is it arrayed against the government of God, and does it permit rebellion against His throne? What sort of gospel is this?" Their consciences would object to a change in the requirements of the gospel.

Sinners do not like the conditions of the gospel: repentance and faith. To hate his sins and to trust in Christ for salvation is too much to ask of him. But suppose the gospel offered to pardon without repentance and faith; the sinner's *conscience* and his common sense would object.

"What?" he would say. "Shall the gospel offer pardon while sinners rebel? Shall people be saved in their sins, without faith in Christ? It is absurd. Should sinners go to a heaven they do not believe in? With no confidence in the testimony of God? A

178

gospel that pretends to save on such conditions must be from hell."

Sinners are at war with themselves. Their *hearts* and *consciences* oppose each other. One subject will please their hearts and offend their consciences; another will satisfy their consciences but arouse the enmity of their hearts. It is impossible to please them. They do not like the means of grace, nor would they be satisfied if any other means were used to save them.

Sinners Are Never Content with the Preacher

If ministers preach pure doctrines of the gospel, and bear down upon the hearts and consciences of men with the claims of God, the hearts of sinners rise in rebellion. "This," say they, "is an abominable doctrine!" But if the minister lets down the high claims of the gospel, their consciences are dissatisfied. If well instructed, the sinner says, "The minister is afraid to tell the truth. He is deceiving the people and leading them down to hell." But should the minister preach a mixture of truth and error, the sinner's heart will oppose the truth and his conscience will condemn the error. He will not be satisfied.

Sinners never appreciate the pastor's manner of preaching. If the sermon is rousing and pointed, the sinner's *heart* rises up against it. If it is cold and dry, the sinner's *conscience* condemns it. He says that the minister is either an enthusiast and a madman or he preaches people to sleep. It is foolish to hope to please him.

The lives of ministers are always a point of irritation for the sinner. If a pastor is determined to know nothing among his people except Jesus Christ and Him crucified, the sinner's heart is filled with indignation. He says the minister is a bigot, not as affable as he ought to be. If the pastor associates with worldly people, takes an interest in politics, reads secular news and books and is cheerful, the sinner's conscience condemns him. He says, "I don't see that he is any better than anybody else. He is not what a minister should be. I like to see a minister confine himself to the duties of his office."

But suppose there is a mixture of right and wrong in a minister's life. Then sinners say he is not at all what he should be; he is sometimes very hot and sometimes very cold. But if the minister lives as he ought, the unrepentant *heart* loathes him; and the *conscience* condemns him.

Sinners Do Not Approve of Christians' Lives

Sinners do not approve of the conduct of Christians. When Christians live holy lives, zealous for the souls of others, they are *morose and unhappy*. But if they are only casual in their Christianity, they are *hypocrites*. The sinner says, "If these are Christians, I want no religion like this." So, if Christians live right or wrong, sinners are not satisfied. Who can please them?

Sinners are displeased if the church exercises discipline and turns out unworthy members. But they are also displeased if they do not do it. If a church allows disorderly and wicked people in their communion, sinners' consciences are opposed to it. They say that church members are all hypocrites to sanction such conduct as this. But if the church rises up and excommunicates offending members, then their hearts are disturbed. They maintain that the church is persecuting some of its best members. Court cases have been brought where the excommunicated members have been advised by the ungodly to prosecute the church for slander. While sinners continue to be inconsistent with themselves, nothing in Christianity can please them. What is right offends their hearts.

PRINCIPLE 42

DO NOT SEEK TO PLEASE SINNERS

Until their consciences are seared as with a hot iron, sinners find it impossible to rest in error. They are always trying to hide behind some refuge of lies. These errors make them feel good and they *want* to believe them. But when the tumult of feeling subsides, and an enlightened conscience gains a hearing, it gives the sentence of condemnation against their favorite heresy. The heart mutinies and starts an internal war, from which the sinner can only escape if he jettisons Scripture and common sense. His tumultuous feelings can then drown the voice of conscience, and for the time being he feels quiet in his sins.

Thus you will see Universalists and heretics of almost every description courting debate. They are unhappy unless they are engaged in some exciting conversation that will drown the voice of conscience. But, if they understand Christianity, they cannot rest quietly in any form of error until by utter violence they have silenced the conscience. It is foolish for them to expect to bring an enlightened conscience to take sides against truth and God. God has not left himself without a witness in the sinner's breast; and no matter how fiercely his warring passions and his desperate heart may mutiny against high heaven, his conscience will write out, sign and seal his death warrant.

Preachers Must Please the Conscience

If a minister preaches with velvet lips the honeyed words of guile, puts darkness for light and light for darkness and plows eloquence like one who can play an instrument well, he conceals the sinner's danger. He says nothing of his guilt, but strengthens the hands of the wicked by promising life. The sinner remarks, "What a charming preacher." He goes home bubbling over with enthusiastic praise for the sermon. But let his feelings subside, let him have time for reflection, and he will change his tune. When speaking the sober dictates of his conscience, he will condemn the preacher and his sermon as intended to deceive rather than to reform and save.

But if he hears a minister who brings the truth of God to bear with impressive pungency upon the hearts and consciences of men, his heart rises in rebellion. He will pour insults upon the minister and declare that he will never hear him preach again. He is ready to quarrel with anyone who will defend the preacher. But let him have time to cool, let conscience gain a hearing, and you will find him speaking a different language. He will return saying, "I may as well go; the man preached the truth, and I may as well hear it as not. I can only respect his honesty." In one of these cases, the sinner speaks the language of his *heart*, and in the other the language of his *conscience*.

A minister who pleases the hearts of sinners cannot commend himself. Many pastors aim at soothing the feelings of the unrepentant in their congregation. They consider the favor of the ungodly an evidence of their wisdom and prudence. If these sinners were converted, they would lose their confidence in such a minister. Their consciences, if enlightened, have never been satisfied with him. They have praised his preaching because he has won their hearts. If their hearts take sides with their consciences, they will probably join another congregation. If they do not, there is reason to fear that they are not truly converted.

Where a minister preaches to the conscience, sinners get angry and go away; but if they are converted, they will come back again and sit under the preaching that used to disturb them.

Christians Cannot Please the Sinner's Heart

When Christians try to gain influence with sinners by lowering the standards of Christianity to make them feel better, they do them no good. For while the Christian pleases their hearts, their consciences condemn them; and it is conscience which they depend on to ultimately judge truth.

Many are attempting to gain influence with the upper class by imitating their lives and habits. They think they can gain access to influence them. But the access and influence they will gain will never do the sinner any good, because the conduct by which it is gained is condemned by the sinner's conscience. It is not a Christian but a worldly influence that they gain. They destroy the confidence of the sinner in their own Christianity.

God speaks and conducts himself so as to commend himself to everyone's conscience. The sinner's heart is entirely opposed to God, but God works to leave himself a witness in the sinner's breast. Conscience will testify for God. The sinner's heart must be reconciled to God or he will be eternally miserable. His judgment will always bear witness that God is right. Unless the heart is brought over to take sides with conscience, the sinner must be damned.

All Christians should do as God does: so live and speak as to commend themselves to the sinner's conscience. If we live like this, however much the sinner may hate us now, it is certain that he must love us or be damned. He must be reconciled to us or God will never be reconciled to him.

PRINCIPLE 43

ALWAYS TAKE GOD'S SIDE

When people are converted, they often are the closest to those Christians whom they most hated before their conversion. Christians that lead holy lives are most likely to be hated by sinners. It often happens that the more Christians warn and rebuke them, the more sinners will hate them. But if the sinners become truly converted, they will have the most confidence in those people who rebuked them because their minds, wills, and hearts are changed. Their conscience took part with the faithful Christian before, and now both heart and conscience approve his character.

The opposite is also true. Converted sinners have the least confidence in those professing Christians with whom they were most intimate before conversion. While unrepentant, those people had been agreeable with them, not because they had so much piety, but because they had so little.

Now that they are converted, they have little confidence in the piety of those with whom they used to share worldly intimacy. They cannot help suspecting that they have no piety at all. In some cases, a person who professed to be a Christian has concealed his light to please the unconverted companion. If the husband or wife becomes converted, there will be little Christian confidence in the other partner. In some cases, converted husbands have said that they have very little confidence in their wife's religion, because she never manifested Christianity enough to disturb them in their sins.

Concealing or evading the claims of the gospel can do the unrepentant no good. If we succeed in pleasing them, we will ruin them. Their hearts must be changed by taking a deep hold upon their consciences. We can only expect to change the heart by laying out the claims of God before the conscience. To conceal the truth from conscience and attempt to win the sinner by a lovely song is to lull him with a siren's voice until he plunges into eternal death.

Convicted sinners often manifest the greatest opposition just before they submit to God. The more conscience is pressed, the more disturbed the sinner generally is. The enlightened conscience obtains firm footing, exerts pressure on the will, and a desperate conflict ensues. In his exasperated feelings, the sinner is sometimes ready to blaspheme the God of heaven. He is most vehement in his enmity while conscience is receiving the truth of God. But when feelings have begun to exhaust their turbulence, the power of truth presented by the Spirit of God exerts such tremendous power through the conscience that the sinner may throw down his weapons and submit to God.

Sinners Test God's Patience

The patience of God in sparing sinners is amazing. Nothing that He does or could do pleases them. If your children treated you in such a manner as sinners treat God, what would you do? How would you feel if you had spoken to their consciences, but their hearts still opposed you. If they were always displeased and murmuring at whatever you did? How little patience the kindest earthly parents have with their children when compared with the longsuffering of God.

God cannot please the sinner. Sinners imagine that if God were as they wanted, they would love Him. They do not realize that if they framed a god to suit their hearts, they would fail to appease their consciences. If God's character could be altered to any degree, it would please the sinner no better than it does now. The only possible way for sinners to be happy is to change themselves rather than expect that God should change.

The need to change our hearts is self-evident. Man's conscience and will are opposed to each other, even where the light of the gospel has never shone. People who follow the inclination of their hearts violate their consciences. People around the world acknowledge it in public by the expiatory sacrifices which they offer to appease their offended gods. However foolish their ideas of God have been, their sacrifices are admission that they have violated their consciences. Not a person on earth can honestly say that he has not violated his conscience.

An enlightened conscience will never change: its testimony will be louder and louder in favor of truth. But there must be a change in the heart or there can be no inward peace.

Most sinners are waiting to hear some satisfying preaching. Sometimes they will go to one revival after another, always waiting to hear something adapted to their case. If they hear preaching that pleases their hearts, their consciences are unimpressed. If it pleases their consciences, their hearts rise up in rebellion.

They wait for something that will please both their consciences and their hearts. But the heart and conscience are at war and there is no use in waiting. To wait for God or anybody else to satisfy you before you are converted is to wait until you are in the depths of hell.

The Inner Conflicts Ignite the Fires of Hell

Can you see the nature of hell's torments? Sinners are often thrown into great agony in this life by the internal struggles of their consciences and hearts. But let the full blaze of eternity's light be poured upon their consciences, and hearts at enmity against God will rise up in rebellion greater than ever before. The conscience will adamantly take the part of God and the heart will supremely hate Him. The conflict will kindle the fires of hell.

Sinners should, therefore, not follow their feelings, but obey the voice of conscience. They attempt to exercise judgment in every other area, but they cease to be reasonable when considering Christianity. They give themselves up to their wicked hearts. They ought to decide promptly not to take another step in the way to death. Why throw up the reins and let passion loose? Why drive with such furious haste to hell? If they do not make up their minds to resist the whole tide of carnal feelings and put themselves under the clear blaze of heaven's light when conscience commands, they must die in their sins.

PART 7

Christian Affinity

"Can two walk together except they be agreed?"
(Amos 3:3).

PRINCIPLE 44

KNOW THE BASIS FOR AGREEMENT

In the Bible, we often find a negative statement spoken forth as a rhetorical question. Amos 3:3 is an example. The prophet asks a question, but his message is clear: two cannot walk together unless they are agreed.

For two to be agreed implies agreement in more than theory or understanding. We often see people who agree in theory, but who differ vastly in feeling and practice. Their minds may embrace the same truths, but their hearts and actions will be very different. Saints and sinners often embrace the same religious creed in theory, but it is plain that they differ widely in their fruits. We have reason to believe that angels and devils *intellectually* believe the same truths, yet they are very differently affected by them.

Different effects are produced in different minds by the same truths because of the different states of the hearts. The same truths will also affect the same mind very differently at different times. This is due to the change in heart over time.

All pleasure and pain, all sin and holiness, have their seat in the heart, in the affections. What we feel when we encounter any truth depends entirely upon the state of our affections at the time. If truth finds a pleasant reception, it excites pleasurable feelings, otherwise it will not please us. If a truth differs from our present feelings and we refuse to change the course of our feelings, we will either view it with indifference, either because it is introduced below the tone of our own feelings or because our affections are engaged in something else, or we will resist it because it opposes our current pursuit.

Everyone experiences this. Present the ardent politician his favorite view of his favorite subject, incite it to burn with eloquence before his mind, and he will be delighted. But change your style and tone, present it in a drier light, and he loses nearly all his interest. Introduce death and judgment and he is shocked and stunned. Force him to think about these and he is disgusted and offended. This loss of interest in his favorite subject is the natural consequence of removing that burning view of it that poured fire through his affections. The disgust that he feels at the change of subject is the natural consequence of presenting something that directly opposed his feelings. Unless he chooses to turn his mind as you change the subject, he will be displeased.

Our Spiritual Affections Dictate Our Response to Everything

If your heart is glowing with thoughts of God, then you are not only averse to the introduction of any other subject, but are uninterested in anything on the same subject that is far below the tone of your affections. Suppose you hear a spiritually cold man preach or pray. While he remains cold you are not interested, for your affections are not fed unless he comes up to your tone. If this does not happen you are perhaps disgusted with his coldness. This will happen naturally.

Suppose, like Paul, you have "great heaviness and continual sorrow in your heart" for dying sinners; that "the Spirit helpeth your infirmities, making intercessions for you, according to the will of God, with groanings that cannot be uttered." In this state of mind, you *cannot be interested* if you hear a person pray without mentioning sinners. You would be grieved and distressed.

Suppose you are lukewarm, carnal and earthly in your affections and you hear someone preach fervently. If you cling to your sins, your affections will not rise. If you refuse to kindle your heart with this subject, even though you may admit every word he says, you will not be pleased. He is above your tone. You are annoyed with the fire and the spirit of the man. While your heart is wrong and he is right, he irritates you.

Those whose affections stand at or near the point of the speaker will not feel disturbed but pleased. Those who are lukewarm will listen to the dull man and say, "Tis pretty well." Their pleasure will be small because their affections are low, but they are pleased. Those with much feeling will listen with grief and pain. They would listen to the ardent man with great interest, while the carnal and cold-hearted would be disturbed with his fire.

People may differ on doctrinal points or belong to different denominations, but will walk together in harmony. It is because they feel alike. Their differences are in a great measure forgotten while they fall in with each other's feelings. They will walk together while they agree in *heart*.

You can see why young converts love to associate with each other and with fervent older saints. They walk together because they agree.

Lukewarm Christians and Sinners Can Agree

Lukewarm Christians and unrepentant sinners have the same difficulties with the way revivals are carried out. We often hear them complain about the preaching and praying. They have the same objections because their affections are nearly the same. The fire and the spirit disturb their frosty hearts. For the time being, they walk together, for in *feeling* they are agreed.

You can see why Christians visiting revivals often raise objections to the way things are done, and sometimes even take sides with the wicked. Often they come from areas where there are no revivals, and they feel reproved and annoyed by the warmth they witness. The praying, preaching and conversation are above their tone of affection. Sometimes they are biased against the denomination or the preacher, or perhaps pride, envy or worldliness chains down their affections so they cannot enter into the spirit of the revival. While their hearts remain wrong, they will naturally complain; and the more spiritual and holy anything is, the more it displeases them.

We do not mean to justify anything that is unscriptural in the way revivals are run; nor do we pretend that everything that offends the sinner is right. We know better. But we do know that anything that pleases a heart while it is wrong must be wrong also; just as one false weight can only be balanced by another just as false. The best things will be the most certain to offend an unholy heart. If this heart could see things as heaven does, it would blaspheme and be filled with the torments of hell. The only remedy is to call upon the sinner to "repent and make him a new heart," then right things will please him.

The person who understands the solemn things of eternity will judge very differently what is right or wrong in revivals than one whose spiritual eyes are almost closed. The man whose heart is breaking for perishing sinners will deem it prudent to "use great plainness of speech," and to deal with sinners in earnestness. He would consider it criminal to do otherwise. The man without a burden for sinners will entertain very different notions of what is prudent.

LUKEWARM CHRISTIANS HATE REVIVALS

Lukewarm Christians and sinners are not disturbed by dull preaching or praying. It does not grip their feelings at all, and therefore neither distresses nor offends them. When wicked hearts are disturbed with pungent preaching in a revival and a dull minister is called upon to preach, they will praise his preaching. During revivals, we often hear sinners and lukewarm Christians wish that their minister would preach as he used to, that he would be himself again. He did not move them before, but now his fire and spirit disturb their carnal slumbers.

Churches May Be Divided by Revival

We can understand why churches are sometimes convulsed by revivals. When revivals are stripped of emotion and become highly spiritual, there are hypocrites in most churches who are disturbed by deep movements of God's Spirit. When only part of the real Christians in a church wake from their slumber and the rest remain carnal, the church is in danger of being torn asunder. As the revived hearts become more spiritual and active, the others must either wake themselves up or become jealous and complain. The spiritual members will continue to grow and the others will not. The widening gap almost insures that the unrepentant will descend until they really have nothing in common with the saints and can no longer walk together with them. A church in this state must urge great searchings of heart in all its members.

We can see why ministers must sometimes move after revivals. It will sometimes happen, without any imprudence on the part of the minister, that many members of his church will not enter into the spirit of a revival. If he feels strongly for his flock and for the honor of his Master, he will press them with truth and annoy them by his spirit. If they refuse God's work, the more powerfully he forces truth, the more he will offend them. In the end he may find it expedient to leave them. This may be as necessary in a minister as it was for Paul to leave places when people were hardened and blasphemed before the multitude.

Sometimes the people may wake up while the shepherd sleeps. This will inevitably destroy their confidence in him.

In either of these cases, the members and the pastor may find themselves unable to walk together, because they are not agreed. In the first case, let the minister obey the command of Christ and "shake off the dust of his feet, for a testimony against them." In the second, let the church shake off their sleepy minister. They are better off without him. "Woe to the shepherds that do feed themselves. Should not the shepherds feed the flocks? Ye feed not the flock. Therefore, O ye shepherds, hear the word of the Lord. Thus saith the Lord God, Behold I am against the shepherds, and I will require my flock at their hand, and cause them to cease from feeding the flock, neither shall the shepherds feed themselves any more. For I will deliver my flock from their mouth, that they may not be meat for them." (Ezekiel 34:2, 3, 9, 10).

Most Will Respond to an Emotional Plea

Carnal people who profess to be Christians and sinners have no difficulty with emotion. It is common in revivals to hear a great deal of opposition to what they term *animal feeling*. It is not strange for it to occur. It is impossible for Christian affection to be excited without exciting the natural emotions. To object to a revival on this account is absurd. In most cases, it is not emotions that give offense. There is perfect agreement between saints and sinners. Sinners have as much natural feeling as saints. Exhort or preach to awaken sympathy and natural feeling, and you will soon see that there is a perfect agreement of feeling among cold and warm-hearted Christians and sinners. They will all weep and no one will be offended—*and I may add, no one will be convicted or converted!* But change your style and preach spiritually, throwing yourself into a direct appeal to the conscience and the heart and their tears will dry up. The carnal and cold-hearted will become uneasy and find themselves offended. So far as natural feeling goes, they walk together, for in this they are agreed. But as soon as feeling becomes spiritual and holy, they can go together no further.

Do you understand why unrepentant sinners cannot enjoy revivals? Because God is in revivals. They hate God, and this is the reason that God commands them to make themselves a new heart. While they have a "carnal mind, which is enmity against God," they hate anything like God, in proportion to how much it bears His image. Hence we see that the more a revival is stripped of emotion and everything wrong, the more it will offend wrong hearts. The better we reveal God, the more it will excite the enmity of carnal hearts.

Why Sinners Do Not Oppose Revival

If carnal-minded people do not oppose a revival, there are three possible causes. Either they are opposed in heart but dare not *openly* fight it, or there is nothing of the Holy Spirit in the revival, or the works of the Holy Spirit are kept out of the sinner's view and covered up in the rubbish of emotion (which often happens from injudicious appeals to the sympathies of the crowd). Anything that keeps the work of the Holy Spirit out of the sinner's view tends to prevent opposition; and everything that exposes the hand of God to the sinner will certainly excite opposition in the unregenerate heart. Excitement which is not opposed by the wicked is either not a revival of Christianity or it is so conducted that sinners do not see the hand of God in it.

The more holy the methods used to promote a revival, the more they are stripped of human infirmity and emotion, the more will they excite the opposition of all wrong hearts. For while a man's heart is wrong, he cannot heartily approve of what is right without contradiction.

It appears that the manner of preaching which calls forth the greatest enmity of the heart is best. However, let no one think that we advocate preaching or malicious means intended to offend. All such things are to be condemned. But we insist that *holy things are offensive to unholy hearts*. While hearts remain unholy, they are pleased with that which is unholy. Reason and the conscience may approve of the truth, but the heart will not.

Hence, we see the folly of those who are laboring to please people whose affections are wrong. They cannot be pleased with anything holy. This shows why so much wrong feeling is often stirred up in revivals of religion.

It is the natural effect of pure revivals to stir up wrong hearts. Revivals on earth stir up hell. They will disturb the same feelings whenever they come in contact with rebellious hearts, whether in or out of the church. Wherever the Holy Spirit comes, the unholy spirit is disturbed. Holiness among saints will naturally stir up wicked feelings in all those whose hearts are wicked. Saints cannot walk together with sinners because they are not agreed; and the more saints become holy in their affections and conduct, the further apart saints and sinners will be. Heaven and hell consist in the different state of the hearts of their respective inhabitants.

PRINCIPLE 46

YOU MUST BE BORN AGAIN

Sinners cannot be saved unless they are born again. It is impossible for sinners and merely professing Christians to be happy with saints and holy angels. Sinners cannot walk with saints here. When sinners become saints and cease to follow the ways of this world, others speak evil of them and think it strange that they no longer run with them. They are offended. They assume that something in saints and revival offends them; but the truth is that the little goodness in saints and that which is the most of God in revivals offends them the most. Were the saints as holy as they will be in heaven, sinners would hate them even more. As saints rise in holiness and sinners sink in sin, they go eternally further apart.

This shows why the lives and preaching of the prophets and apostles, as well as the revivals of the early church, met with so much more violent opposition from carnal, professing believers and from ungodly sinners than is offered to preachers and revivals these days. They were more holy in their lives and words than preachers and Christians in these days.

We cannot deny that the saints of those days had trials of cruel mocking and scourging, of bonds and imprisonment. They were stoned, sawn in half, tempted, and slain with the sword. They wandered about in sheep and goatskins, destitute, afflicted and tormented, of whom the world was not worthy.

Nor can we deny that the preaching of the prophets, of

Christ, His apostles and of early ministers was opposed with great bitterness by many professing saints and multitudes of ungodly sinners, more than that of any preacher of today. Those who professed religion were often leaders of the opposition, stirring up the Romans to crucify Jesus and afterwards persecuting and killing His saints, and crucifying His apostles. Even the religious teachers and doctors of the law endeavored to prejudice the multitude against the Savior and to prevent them from listening to His teaching. They said, "He hath a devil and is mad." Later, they led the way in opposing the apostles in revivals.

"Turning the World Upside Down"

Those revivals attracted so much attention that the apostles were accused of "turning the world upside down" and sinners often bitterly hardened themselves against the preaching of Christ and His apostles. They were "filled with great wrath," and opposed with such bitterness that Christ told His apostles to "let them alone." In some places where the apostles preached, some were so hardened that they "contradicted and blasphemed, and spake evil of this way," so much that the apostles were forced to go to other places, sometimes under very humiliating circumstances, escaping only with their lives.

These are facts we need not blush to meet; they are easily accounted for by the principle contained in the text from Amos, "Can two walk together except they be agreed?" There is no evidence that the prophets, Christ or His apostles were imprudent, unholy men, whose preaching was overbearing or whose manner was wrong in calling sinners to repentance. The prophets were holy in their lives and bold and faithful in delivering their messages, and Christ was so clear and personal in His preaching and so entirely "separate from sinners" in His life that the wicked were opposed. The ways the apostles promoted revival were holier and less adulterated with fleshly ways than they are now. There was less emotional plea and hypocritical suavity of manner intended to court the applause of the ungodly. "Renouncing the hidden things of dishonesty, not walking in craftiness, nor handling the word of God deceitfully," they preached, "not with the enticing words of man's wisdom," but "with great plainness of speech" so that the ungodly in the church and out of it were filled with wrath.

Stephen was so holy and piercing in his address that the elders of Israel "gnashed upon him with their teeth." But this is not evidence that he was imprudent. The fact that revivals today are much more silent and gradual than they were on the day of Pentecost, because they create much less noise and opposition among cold, carnal Christians (who only profess spirituality) and ungodly sinners, does not prove that the theory of revival is better understood now than it was then; nor that Christians engaged in revivals are more prudent than the apostles. To suppose this would show great spiritual pride in us. The human heart has not changed, nor is the character of God less offensive "to the carnal mind."

Revival Demands a Clear Message of Holiness

The prophets, Christ, His apostles and the early saints were holier, bolder, clearer and more pungent in their preaching and less conformed to this crazy world. In one word, they were more like heaven than we are. These are the reasons why they were hated more than we are, why their preaching and praying gave so much more offense than ours. Revivals in their days were freer from carnal policy, management that tends to keep the naked hand of God out of the sinner's view. These are the reasons why they made so much more noise than we witness in these days. They stirred up so much of earth and hell to oppose them that they turned the world upside down. They made known that "men could not serve God and Mammon," that "if any man will live godly in Christ Jesus, he shall suffer persecution." They made it understood that if "ministers pleased men, they were not the servants of Christ." The church and world could not walk together for they were not agreed.

Let us not be puffed up, imagining that we are wiser than Christ and the apostles; able to get the attention of carnal, professing Christians and sinners whose "carnal mind is enmity against God," without calling forth their opposition. But let us realize that if our lives and preaching cause less opposition than the apostles', it is because we are less holy than they were. If we walk with the lukewarm and ungodly, or they with us, it is because we are agreed; for two cannot walk together except they be agreed.*

---

*As a Christian or minister laboring for revival, expect opposition from sinners, the ungodly, carnal minded people who profess to be Christians. Expect opposition and do not be discouraged. Pray without ceasing. Study and apply God's Word to your life and the lives of others. Obey God, and find like-minded Christians so you can mutually encourage one another. Some will be born again through your efforts. Some will live holy lives, because of your work.

PART 8

Stewardship

"Give an account of thy stewardship"
(Luke 16:2).

PRINCIPLE 47

ALL ARE GOD'S STEWARDS

A steward is employed to transact the business of another as his agent. His duty is to promote the interests of his employer. At any time, the employer may call him to account for the manner in which he has done business, always with the possibility of removing the steward.

A major intention of the parable in Luke 16 is to teach that all are God's stewards. The Bible declares that the silver and gold are His; that He is, in the highest sense, the proprietor of the universe. All men are mere stewards, employed by Him for doing His business, and required to do all for His glory. Everything, even their eating and drinking, are to be done for His glory, that they may be strengthened for peak performance for His business.

God treats people as stewards. He removes them from their office at His pleasure, and disposes of the property in their hands without their consent. If they were owners, rather than stewards, He could not do this.

If we are God's stewards, we must account to God for our time. God created us, keeps us alive, and our time is His. If you employed a steward and paid him for his time, would you not expect him to use that time in your service? Would it not be fraud for him, while in your pay, to spend his time in idleness or in private interests? If he were often idle, that would be bad enough; but suppose he wholly neglected your business, and when called to account and censured for not doing his duty, he said, "Why, what have I done?" It would be wickedness for which he deserved to be punished.

If you are an unrepentant sinner, you have wholly neglected God's business. You have remained idle in His vineyard, or have only been attending to your own private interests. Are you ready to see what you have done? Are you not deceitful to ignore the business of your employer for the sake of your own?

Sinners Are as Rebellious Stewards Opposed to the Master

But suppose your steward employed his time in *opposing* your interests, using your capital and time to accomplish tasks directly opposed to your goals. Is this not great dishonesty? It would be ridiculous for him to account himself an honest man. Would you not be obliged to call him to account? And would not anyone who approved his actions share his guilt? It would be your duty to separate yourself from this villain and announce that you will have nothing to do with what he has done.

How shall God deal with you, if you employ your time in opposing His interests? If you use His capital to directly oppose the business for which He has employed you? Are you not ashamed to say you are an honest man; and does God have any choice but to call you to account? He is constrained to make you a public example that the universe may know how much He abhors your crimes!

Stewards are bound to give account of their talents, of the powers of their minds. Suppose you educated a man to be your steward, supported the entire cost of his schooling, and then he either neglected to use his mind in your service or he used his cultivated intellect for the promotion of his own interests. Is this not villainy? God created your mind, has provided your education, and has trained you up for His service. Is your mind idle; or are you using your intellect to promote your own interests, then asking what you have done to deserve the wrath of God?

But suppose your steward should use his education in opposition to your interest, and use all the powers of his mind to destroy the very interest for which he was educated, and which he is employed to sustain. Would you not look upon his conduct as marked with horrid guilt? And do you, sinner, employ the powers of your mind, and whatever education God may have given you, in opposing His interest, perverting His truth, scattering "fire-brands, arrows, and death" all around you, and think to escape His curse? Shall not the Almighty be avenged upon such a wretch?

A Steward Must Give Account of His Influence

A steward is bound to give an account of his influence on those around him. Suppose you employed a steward, educated him until he possessed great talents, put a large amount of money into his hands, exalted him high in society and placed him in circumstances to exert an immense influence in the commercial community. If he refused or neglected to exert his influence for your interests, would this not be wrong?

But suppose he exerted all his influence against you, taking sides against you with everything he had, even the money you had entrusted to him. He would be anything but innocent of wrong!

If you are an unrepentant sinner, you are not only neglecting to use the influence God has given you to build up His kingdom, but you are using it to oppose His interests and glory. Don't you deserve the damnation of hell? Perhaps you are rich, educated, have great influence in society, and are refusing to use any of this to save souls. You are using all your character, talents, influence and example to drag everyone within the sphere of your influence down to the gates of hell.

PRINCIPLE 48

YOU MUST GIVE AN ACCOUNT OF YOUR SOUL

You must account for the manner in which you use the property in your possession. Suppose your steward refused to use your capital for the promotion of your interests. Suppose he treated it as his own and used it for his own interests, to gratify his lusts, or to enhance his family's status by giving large portions to his daughters or to the lusts and pride of his sons. All this time your business was suffering financially. Suppose that this steward, with the purse strings of your wealth, had neglected to supply the necessities for your multitudes of other servants as he was charged to do, even though their lives depended on these supplies. What would you think of such wickedness? You entrusted him with your money and the care of your other servants, but through his neglect, they are all dead men.

God Must Protect His Interests

You have God's money in your hands, and are surrounded by God's children whom He commands you to love as you do yourself. God might, with perfect justice, have given His property to them instead of you. The world is full of poverty, desolation, and death; hundreds and millions are perishing in body and soul. God calls you to act as His steward for their salvation; to use all the property in your possession to achieve the highest level of happiness among your fellow creatures. The Macedonian cry comes from the four winds of heaven, "Come over and help us;" COME OVER AND HELP US; and yet you refuse to help. You hoard the wealth in your possession, live in luxury, and let your neighbor go to hell. What can describe your guilt?

Suppose your servant, when you called him to account, should say, "I have acquired this property by my own hard work"? You would have to answer, "You have used my capital to do it, and my time for which I have paid you. Therefore, the money you have gained is mine." When God calls you to use the property in your possession for Him, do you say it is yours, that you have obtained it on your own? Whose time have you used, and whose talents and means? God created you. He has sustained you. He has prospered you. Your time is His. You have no right to say that the wealth you have is yours. It is His and you are bound to use it for His glory. You betray His trust if you do not so employ it.

If your clerk takes just a little of your money, his character is ruined and you brand him a villain. But sinners take all of God's money they can get and use it for themselves. It would be wrong if God did not call you to account and punish you for filling your pockets with His money.

Sinners Have No Right to Go to Hell

You have no right to go to hell. God has a right to your soul. Your going to hell would injure the whole universe. It would injure hell because it would increase its torments, and it would injure heaven because it would cheat it out of your services. Who will take your place in singing praises to God? Who will contribute your share to the happiness of heaven?

Suppose you had a steward whom you had saved from death, had educated at great expense, and then he willfully threw that life away. Has he a right to dispose of a life so valuable to you? God has made your soul, sustained and educated you so that you are now able to render Him important services and to glorify Him forever. Have you a right to go to hell, to throw away your soul, and thus rob God of your service? Have you a right to render hell more miserable and heaven less happy, and thus injure God and all the universe?

Do you still say, "It is nobody's business but my own if I lose my soul?" But it is everybody's business. A person might just as well bring a contagious disease into a city and spread death all around, insisting that it was nobody's business but his own.

You must account for the souls of others. God commands you to work with Him in converting the world. He needs your services, for He saves souls only through His people. If souls are lost or the gospel is not spread over the world, sinners may blame Christians because they are bound to carry out the cause of Christ, to give, to pray for a lost world and to pull sinners out of the fire. Who has absolved you from these duties? You lie as a stumbling block in the way of other sinners. Thus, instead of helping to save a world, all your actions help to send souls to hell.

You must give an account of the ideas you entertain and tell others. God's kingdom is to be built up by truth and not by error. Your ideas will have an important bearing upon the influence you exert over those around you.

The Steward Has Rules of Action

Suppose your steward's business required that he follow strict rules concerning the manner and principles involved, knowledge of your will and of his duty. You gave him a written set of rules to govern his conduct in all the affairs with which he was entrusted. If he neglected to read those rules, or perverted their plain meaning and led others in the way of disobedience, would this not be criminal, deserving severe reproof?

God has given you rules for your conduct. In the Bible you have a plain revelation of His will for your heart and all your actions. Do you neglect or pervert it, and lead others with you in the way of disobedience and death; and then call yourself an honest man?

You must account for your opportunities for doing good. If you employed a steward to transact your business, you would expect him to take advantage of the market and use every opportunity to promote your interests. Suppose at the busy seasons of the year, he was idle or involved with his private affairs, without an eye to the most favorable opportunities for your interests. Would you not demand, "Give an account of thy stewardship, for thou mayest be no longer steward?" Have you always neglected opportunities to serve God, or to warn your fellow sinners, or to promote revivals and advance the interests of truth? Have you involved yourself only with your own interests, and entirely neglected the interests of your employer? You are a wretch. How can you escape the damnation of hell?

PRINCIPLE 49

BUSINESS IS SPIRITUAL

The business of this world can be a snare that drowns men's souls. Sinners transact business to promote their own interests, and thus they act dishonestly, defrauding God, grieving the Holy Spirit and promoting their own sensuality, pride and death. If men considered themselves God's stewards, they would not lie or cheat or work on the Sabbath to make money for Him. God did not create this world to be a snare for people; He designed it to be a delightful abode for them—but how perverted it has become!

If everyone realized they were doing God's business, it would have no tendency to wean their souls from Him or to banish Him from their thoughts. When holy Adam tended God's garden, was his mind tempted to banish the thought of God? If your gardener were busy in your presence all day, dressing your plants, asking your opinion and doing your pleasure continually, would this tend to banish you from his thoughts? If you were busy all day seeking God's glory and transacting all your business for Him, acting as His steward, knowing that His eyes were upon you, you would have no tendency to turn your thoughts from God.

Suppose a mother, whose son was in a distant land, was busy all day getting clothes, books and necessities together to send to him. Would her work have a tendency to divert her mind from her absent son? Consider yourself God's steward doing His business. If you are seeking His interests and His glory, and consider all your possessions, including your time and your talents, His, then the busier you are in His service, the more God will be present in all your thoughts.

Idleness is a Snare for the Soul

Do you see why idleness is a snare for the soul? A person who is idle becomes dishonest. He forgets his responsibility, refuses to serve God, and gives himself up to the temptations of the devil. The idle person tempts the devil to tempt him.

Do you see the error in saying that people cannot attend to business and religion at the same time? *A man's business ought to be part of his Christianity!* He cannot be a Christian and idle. He must have some business to be holy, and if it is performed from a right motive, his business is as necessary as prayer, going to church or reading his Bible. Anyone who argues against this is a confessed deceiver; for no one can believe that honest employment pursued for God's glory is inconsistent with biblical religion. The objection tells us that he considers his business either unlawful, or that he pursues it dishonestly. If his employment is wicked, he must relinquish it; if it is honest but pursued in wickedness, he must change his ways. In either case, he will lose his soul unless he repents. A busy life is best for Christians, since it exercises their graces and makes them strong.

Our Losses Are God's Losses

Most people do not consider themselves God's stewards. This is evident from the fact that they consider their business losses as their own. Imagine that some of your debtors failed, and your clerks spoke of it as their loss. It would sound ridiculous. Is it not just as ridiculous for you to worry over any of your Lord's debtors failing? Is it your loss or His? If you have done your duty and taken proper care of His property, any losses are not yours but His. You need not be frightened that God will go bankrupt. If you act as God's steward or clerk, you should not think of any loss as your own loss.

It is ridiculous, in one sense, to call institutions for the extension of the Redeemer's kingdom "charitable." If you gave your steward orders to give a sum of money for the benefit of the poor in a certain place, this would be charity for you, but not in him. It would be ridiculous for him to pretend that the charity was his. Christian institutions are the charities of God and not of man. The funds are God's, and it is His requirement that they be spent according to His directions to relieve the misery or promote the happiness of our fellowmen. To consider the charities as the gifts of men is to maintain that the funds belong to men and not to God. To call them charitable institutions, in the sense in which they are usually spoken of, is to say that men do God a favor. They give Him their money and consider Him as an object of charity.

PRINCIPLE 50

YOU MUST ACCOUNT FOR YOUR WAY OF LIFE

Imagine that a group of merchants with immense capital employed a number of agents to transact their business in India. It would sound ridiculous if the agents claimed the funds as their property and considered a servant carrying orders to write checks on those funds a beggar. It would appear even more foolish if they formed a charitable society to pay these drafts, making themselves "life members" by paying a few dollars of their employers' money into a common fund, and directing any requests for funds to the treasurer. What do you think of yourself when you talk of supporting charitable institutions as if God, the owner of the universe, were soliciting charity, and His servants were beggars? We can wonder that God does not take such men and put them in hell, and then execute His plans for converting the world with the money He had loaned them.

Stewards Do Not Give Charity from Their Employer's Funds

It is no less ridiculous for us to suppose that giving from the funds in our hands is actually charity. It must be born in mind that the money is not ours. We are God's stewards, paying out on His orders.

When the servants of the Lord request funds, you can pay

from the money in your possession into His treasury to defray the expenses of His government. Why do you call it your own and say you can't spare it? What do you mean by calling the agents beggars and saying you are sick of seeing so many? Suppose your steward called your agents beggars and said he was sick of so many beggars? Would you not reprimand him and let him see that the property in his possession was yours and not his?

Do you see the great wickedness of people hoarding property, and at death leaving part of it to the church? What a will! To leave God half of His own property! Suppose a clerk made a will leaving his employer part of his own company! Yet this is called piety. Christ is not a beggar. But the church is filled with charitable donations and legacies to Jesus Christ.

Do you see the wickedness of laying up money for your children, and why that money is a curse to them? Suppose your steward laid up your money for his children? Would you not consider him a thief? How dare you take God's money and lay it up for your children while the world is sinking into hell? But will you say, "Is it not my duty to provide for my own household?" It is your duty to suitably provide for them; but what is suitable provision? Give them the education you can for the service of God. Make all necessary provision for their real needs "till they become of sufficient age to provide for themselves." Then if you see them serving God and their generation, give them all the advantages for doing this in your power. But to make them rich, to feel their pride, to enable them to live in luxury or ease, to allow your daughters to spend their time in dress, idleness, gossiping, and effeminacy, you have no right. It is defrauding God, ruining your own soul, and greatly endangering theirs.

Unrepentant sinners will be eternally disgraced in the end. They will appear as wicked stewards before an injured God and an injured universe. They have despised God's laws and warred with the interests of the universe. The profession of a person who claims to be a Christian will not cover his selfishness and vile hypocrisy. If you have defrauded God, spent His money upon your lusts and spoken of His servants as beggars, what can save you? How do you dare to pray? How do you dare sit at the communion table or even profess the religion of Jesus Christ if you have set private interests before His glory.

A True Test of Christian Character

This is a true test of Christian character. True Christians consider themselves God's stewards. They act for God, live for Him, transact business for Him, eat and drink for His glory, live and die to please Him. But sinners and hypocrites live for themselves. They account their time, talents and influence as their own and dispose of them all for their own private interests, and thus drown themselves in perdition.

At the judgment, we are informed that Christ will say to those who are accepted, "Well done, good and faithful servants." Could He say this to you, "Well done, good and faithful servant; thou hast been faithful over a few things": over the things committed to your charge? He will not pronounce false judgment. Those not accepted will be thrust down to hell. God will soon call you to give account of your stewardship. Have you been faithful to God, to your own soul and the souls of others? If not, repent, *repent now* of all your wickedness. Lay hold of the hope that is set before you. Don't you realize that you need the blood of Jesus Christ to cover your sins? A voice even now cries in your ears, "Give an account of thy stewardship, for thou mayest be no longer steward."